Shp Retirement Road Map

YOUR MAP TO
FINANCIAL FREEDOM

Derek L. Gregoire, Keith W. Ellis Jr.
and Matthew C. Peck, CFP®, CIMA®

SHP Financial
PLYMOUTH, MASSACHUSETTS

Copyright © 2020 by Derek L. Gregoire, Keith W. Ellis Jr. and Matthew C. Peck.

All rights reserved. No part of this publication may be reproduced, distributed or transmitted in any form or by any means, including photocopying, recording or other electronic or mechanical methods, without the prior written permission of the publisher, except in the case of brief quotations embodied in critical reviews and certain other noncommercial uses permitted by copyright law. For permission requests, write to the publisher at the address below.

The case studies/examples and results included in this book are for illustration purposes only and may not be typical. The results shown will not be achieved for all clients or even for any client. Results for each client will differ depending on the client's situation. They should not be considered specific investment advice, do not take into consideration your specific situation, and are not intended to make an offer or solicitation for the sale or purchase of any securities or investment strategies. **Investments involve risk and are not guaranteed.** Additionally, no legal or tax advice is being offered. If legal or tax advice is needed a qualified professional should be engaged.

Derek L. Gregoire, Keith W. Ellis Jr. and Matthew C. Peck /SHP Financial
225 Water Street, Building C
Suite C210
Plymouth, MA 02360
www.shpfinancial.com

Book layout ©2013 BookDesignTemplates.com

Ordering information:
Quantity sales. Special discounts are available on quantity purchases by corporations, associations and others. For details, contact the address above.

SHP Retirement Road Map/ Derek L. Gregoire, Keith W. Ellis Jr. and Matthew C. Peck. —3rd ed.
ISBN 9798636013983

Contents

Introduction i
Income Planning 1
    Focusing on the Wrong Number 2
    Four Key Parts to Any Income Plan 3
    The Evolution of the Income Plan 14
    4 Percent Rule — Is It Still a Safe Withdrawal Rate? .. 16
    Annuities: To Buy or Not to Buy? 20
    Lessons From 2008 21
    Conclusion: Retirement Is Not the Time to Gamble 23
Investment Planning 27
    Misunderstanding Risk 28
    Which Vehicle to Use? 30
    Active vs. Strategic Money Management 34
Tax Planning 37
    Are Taxes on the Rise? 38
    Tax Planning Strategies to Buy Out Uncle Sam 39
    Roth IRA Conversions 39
    More into Post-Tax Dollars 40
    Tax Loss Harvesting 40
    SECURE Act of 2019 42
    What to Do With Excess RMDs 43
    Leveraging Life Insurance 45
    Tax Considerations for a Surviving Spouse 46
    Conclusion: Take a Team Approach 47
Health Care Planning 49
    Managing the Costs of Health Care Before Age 65 49
    Managing the Costs of Health Care After Age 65 — Medicare 50

- Rising Cost of Health Care 53
- Long-Term Care 54
- Case Example 64
- Addressing the Long-Term Care Gap 65

Legacy Planning 67
- Avoiding Probate 67
- Estate Taxes 70
- Capital Gains Taxes and Step-Up Cost Basis 71
- Life Insurance and ILITs in Estate Planning 71
- Conclusion 73

Building Your Own Road Map 75
- Paving the Way to a Beautiful Retirement 80

I dedicate this book to my wife, Diana. No matter how difficult my job can be, nothing can compare to the enormous task of raising our four children and running the household. Although it may not appear in paperback form, I am so proud of everything she has accomplished.
-Matthew C. Peck, CFP®, CIMA®

I dedicate this book to my wife, Kylene, and to all of our clients who have trusted us with their life savings and financial planning needs. Many people took a chance on us in our early years, before we had an established firm. I cannot ever extend my appreciation enough for their believing in us those many years ago. Looking forward to many more great years together!
-Derek L. Gregoire

I dedicate this book to my wife of seven years, Maura, for all of the hard work she does with our two boys, Aiden and Keith Ellis III (a.k.a. Trey, and our daughter, Emory). I also would like to dedicate this book to the many families that have trusted us to help them build their retirement plans. Without them, none of what we do is possible. Thank you so much, and I look forward to serving you for many years to come.
-Keith W. Ellis Jr.

The SHP Financial Mission

With the clients' best interest as our beacon, we strive to build the foundation for their personal and financial goals; yet this is only possible with a perfect alignment of company and client. Their gain is our gain. Their loss is our loss. Whether it is the independent and innovative financial strategies or the customer service that is above and beyond industry expectations, when we see the world through our clients' eyes and our separate goals become one, then we have the opportunity to truly change lives for the better.

Introduction

Time and again, we talk to people who are going through a fundamental shift in their lives. No, it is not from child to adolescent, nor from single to married. It's not even from wife to mother. Of course, these are all big changes in one's life, but they will not be the biggest changes. The most significant change happens when one transitions from being in the workforce to being in retirement.

Today's retirees are redefining the meaning of retirement. They're living longer. They are extremely active. They want their golden years to be filled with learning new things, taking on new challenges, starting businesses, spending quality time with their families and traveling the world. But, as they look forward to leaving the workforce and starting out on these new adventures, the rite of passage can often be daunting for today's retirees. There's a multitude of planning that needs to be done prior to making the shift into the nonworking life. Beyond the emotional shift, the most significant piece is protecting and planning for problems that could come up with finances.

When it comes to finances, we call your working years the "accumulation phase" of your life. This is when you're working and setting aside, or accumulating, money for retirement. Whereas, when you retire, you shift from accumulating wealth to distributing it. We call that time the "distribution phase." This is when you are drawing down on your savings to supplement the income you no longer have. When it comes to managing your money, the distribution years are a whole new ball game.

According to a MarketWatch article, "Is your advisor still right for you?," the author says "the distribution phase and the planning that goes along with it makes the accumulation phase look like child's play."[1] Making the transition to retirement requires a complete mind shift, a change in the way you think about money and — in particular — your investments. In our profession, we sit with people every day who have worked their whole lives, saving for the day they can walk out of the workforce on their terms. However, all too often, we hear stories of people whose retirement dreams were crushed because they failed to readjust their way of thinking when it came to their money or their investment philosophy. Once you are entering into your retirement years, you're no longer working to put money away. In fact, in financial planning circles, we see retirement as unemployment. Now, your money is working for you. That is why, in order to have success in retirement, you need to have a plan — a road map — created and managed by a financial professional who specializes in the distribution phase of retirement.

When you fail to have an adequate retirement plan, you put your retirement dreams at risk. Throughout this book, we'll be providing hypothetical stories of clients and although they are fictitious, their situations are very common. For example, back in 2009, we had a couple come to us looking for help. Michael, an electrician, was 65 and ready to retire that year. His wife, Susan, was in the process of selling her small day care business,

---

[1] Glenn Ruffenach. MarketWatch. May 5, 2011. "Is Your Adviser Still Right for Your Retirement?" http://www.marketwatch.com/story/is-your-adviser-still-right-for-your-retirement-1304621779712.

was 64 and was also looking to start the retirement they had dreamed of.

When we sat down for our first meeting, Michael said to us, "We probably should have been here years ago, but life got in the way and we just never found the time." They procrastinated, just like most of us do. They should have started putting together a plan back in 2007, or better yet 2005, if they wanted to retire in 2009. Unfortunately, they never got around to it. Although, when it comes to mapping out your plans for retirement, it's always better late than never.

In 2007, after 40 long years of working, Michael and Susan had managed to save $700,000 for retirement. Had they made a plan for that money back in 2007, we could have provided them with a plan that would have allowed them to retire with secure, predictable income to cover all of their living expenses. Unfortunately, due to their procrastination, they left their $700,000 in a portfolio that was too aggressively invested in the market and lacked diversification. It was set up for the accumulation stage. When the market crashed in 2008, they lost 40 percent of their assets, or $280,000. $280,000! Now their $700,000 is only $420,000. If you equate that to working years, that's 40 percent of their work life. So, say Michael worked for 30 years, that's 12 out of the 30 years… gone.

By the time they came to us, the plan they had hoped for was no longer achievable. Their total Social Security was $60,000 a year, and what they needed to cover their living expenses was $90,000 a year, not factoring in taxes. So, instead of fully retiring, Michael now had to continue working part-time to supplement his income. If they had not procrastinated and had come to us, or to any credible financial planner, to put together their retirement plan years earlier using the $700,000 they originally had, they could have been given a predictable and reliable income of $90,000 per year, with inflation. Instead, he now has to work part-time to supplement that gap.[2]

Michael and Susan's story is just one of many we've seen over the years. That's why it is so important to make sure that, once you are less than 10 years away from retirement, or are already retired, it's crucial that you see a financial professional who specializes in the distribution phase of retirement, someone who can work with you to put together a well-thought-out and comprehensive plan regardless of the market conditions.

Any good retirement and financial plan should consist of at least five fundamental elements — all of which are a part of the planning process at SHP Financial known as the *Retirement Road Map®*. Our *Retirement Road Map®* consists of an income plan, an investment plan or strategy based on the amount of risk you are comfortable with, a tax plan for you and your next generation, a health care plan and a legacy plan. Throughout this book, we will cover each area in greater detail so that you will have a guide on what factors to consider when creating your own road map to get you to and through retirement.

---

[2] The case studies/examples and results included in this book are for illustration purposes only and may not be typical. The results shown will not be achieved for all clients or even for any client. Results for each client will differ depending on the client's situation. They should not be considered specific investment advice, do not take into consideration your specific situation, and are not intended to make an offer or solicitation for the sale or purchase of any securities or investment strategies. **Investments involve risk and are not guaranteed.** Additionally, no legal or tax advice is being offered. If legal or tax advice is needed, a qualified professional should be engaged.

CHAPTER ONE

Income Planning

What are your dreams for retirement? Or, another way of saying it is: If money wasn't an issue, what would you do? Do you want to travel? Take on a new hobby? Spend time spoiling your grandkids? No matter what your idea of the perfect retirement is, there is one thing you will need more than anything else to make your dreams come true: income. When you're working, you don't need an income plan, you're income is your work. In retirement, although you may have some of the most rewarding times of your life, you are technically unemployed and need a replacement for your paycheck. You need a plan for cash flow that will exceed expenses. Without this income plan, there is no retirement.

Let's think about this for a moment. When you retire, you are potentially entering into 25 to 30 years of unemployment with typically no guaranteed paycheck besides Social Security, unless you are one of the lucky few who still have a pension. That's why it is so important to have a plan for generating income in retirement.

Focusing on the Wrong Number

Unfortunately, one of the biggest pitfalls that people face is focusing on the wrong number. So many people are told to accumulate and focus on a number for their retirement savings. They just chose a number as if drawing one out of a hat. Whether it is $500,000, $1 million or $5 million, many folks are focused on a random number that they think they need to save before they make the decision to retire.

What we are saying is that instead of choosing a random number to focus on, what you should be focused on is determining how much income you will need to live the lifestyle you want. The most important number is really a ratio or balance between income and expenses. It's surprising how common it is for people to overlook this point and to work with a number that may not make sense for them.

For example, we had a client who made this mistake. After meeting with us, he realized that he could have retired years earlier. Dave worked in commercial real estate, and, when he first sat down with us back in 2009, he told us a story that would change the way we looked at income.

"I'm 66 years old. I have worked my whole life. I have saved up $750,000 and I just knew I needed to get to a million dollars," Dave said. "In 2008, I calculated that if I worked for three more years with aggressive stock growth and contributions to my retirement accounts, I figured I'd have a million dollars."

Unfortunately, Dave never hit his $1 million mark. We all know too well what happened back in 2008. Shortly after he made his plan to save for three more years, the stock market crashed and Dave's $750,000 dropped to $475,000. While $475,000 may still seem like a lot of money to many of us, it's a painful loss to take, especially when you have worked so hard for so long to accumulate that nest egg.

The worst part of this story is that it did not have to happen. When Dave came in on that day in 2009 and shared his story, we asked him why it was so important for him to save $1 million. Where did he get that number from? He didn't know. He just picked a magic number to get to, based upon on what he had "heard."

In reality, if he had retired at 66, when he had $750,000 and did the proper planning, he would have been all set for the rest of his life. When we analyzed his lifestyle goals and established his income sources and expenses for retirement, he never needed to strive for $1 million in the first place. Now, due to the loss he suffered at the end of 2008, he is still working part-time to cover his expenses.

It's not about hitting a magic number. It's about itemizing your expenses, determining how much income you will have coming in from Social Security and any possible pension, then isolating what the gap is and how much you will need from your assets each year to live the lifestyle you want. Once the income gap is established and addressed, you are now set up for the next stages: investments, taxes, health care and legacy. As you go through the remaining chapters in this book, you'll see components of the income plan appear, since it's the foundation of your retirement. Everything about it is interrelated — creating one well-rounded, holistic retirement plan. If this all sounds complicated to you, don't worry. Our team at SHP Financial can do all the heavy lifting for you. That's our passion. We work hard for you, so you can enjoy your retirement years.

Four Key Parts to Any Income Plan

There are four key components to any well-rounded retirement income plan: Social Security maximization, income and expense analysis, a spousal income plan and an inflation plan.

1. Maximizing Social Security

When looking at your retirement income plan it is important to maximize every source of income available to you, and it starts with Social Security. We've heard from people in the past who say they want to take their benefits as soon as possible. They're not sure how long they are going to live, so they want to start taking their benefits right away in order to get as much of the benefit as they can while they're alive. What many people don't know is that there is a significant amount of planning you can do to optimize your Social Security benefits. There are many, many different withdrawal strategies for Social Security that can increase the amount you receive, such as delaying benefits or looking at your spousal options.

First and foremost, you can significantly increase the amount of benefits you receive over your lifetime by simply delaying taking your benefits. Social Security retirement benefits are increased by a certain percentage (depending on your date of birth) if you delay your retirement beyond full retirement age. This benefit increase applies until you reach the age of 70.

The increase in benefits by delaying your Social Security can be substantial. For some people, it could be as much as 8 percent. That's a great return on your money! The best part is that it is guaranteed by the federal government. If you have retirement assets saved that you can use for expenses, it could be a good idea to delay your Social Security for a few years to accumulate that growth and increase that portion of your qualified income. What is interesting is that it may not be to delay your payments all of the way to 70, it could be 67 or 68; however, taking it early doesn't work out for an average lifespan.

Increases for Delayed Retirement[3]	
Year of birth	**Yearly rate of increase**
1933-1934	5.5%
1935-1936	6.0%
1937-1938	6.5%
1939-1940	7.0%
1941-1942	7.5%
1943 or later	8.0%

Financial advisors who focus on a holistic, well-rounded approach to retirement planning, such as SHP Financial, will have access to sophisticated Social Security planning software that shows different "what-if" scenarios to help clients make well-informed decisions about their benefits. While no one knows exactly how long they are going to live, this software can take basic knowledge of one's situation and pinpoint the best strategies for obtaining the most money you can in your lifetime. You get to make this decision only once and without a plan or some number crunching, you're really just making the decision on a wing and a prayer.

Here are thoughts to consider in regard to Social Security:

a) **Health**: Health is a key factor to consider in your Social Security plan. "How long am I going to live?" Such an existentialist question is impossible to answer. When you are considering your decision as to whether to start your Social Security income, it is best to give yourself a frank and honest

---

[3] Social Security Administration. "Retirement Planner: Delayed Retirement Credits." https://www.ssa.gov/planners/retire/delayret.html.

assessment. Think about your current health and the longevity of your parents. Thanks to advancements in medicine, what was killing our parents may now be treated, if it is detected early. Because of developments in medical technology, and because of better lifestyle habits and more exercise, people are living longer these days. With a reasonable amount of logic and common sense, you should be able to know how confident you feel about living until age 77.

b) ***Break-even age:*** Your "break-even" age is the age to which you would have to live in order for the numbers to fall in your favor. If you elected to take your Social Security benefits at age 62 instead of waiting until age 70, for example, to what age would you have to live in order to receive more than you paid into the system during your working years?

Remember the number 81. Putting aside the cost of living increases, by taking your Social Security at age 62, you are ahead of the game and are receiving more money during the first 19 years. On average, after age 81, the precipitous slide begins. You now start withdrawing less money compared to what you could have if you had delayed benefits. The longer you live, the worse the decision to take early benefits becomes.

Consider this chart that maps the potential benefit earnings at different starting years.[4] Unequivocally, the later you start your payments, the more you earn each year past age 77. And this is with no cost-of-living adjustment included.

---

[4] Social Security Administration. "Benefit Calculators." https://www.ssa.gov/oact/quickcalc/.

When Will You Break Even?

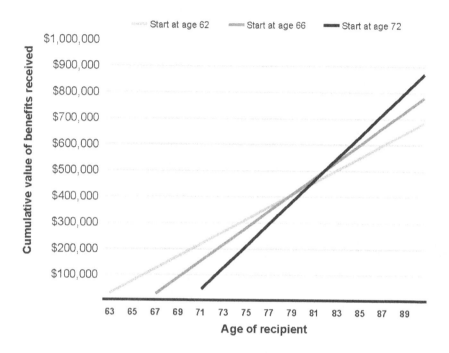

Estimates based on data from ssa.gov, shown in today's dollars, using SSA's "Quick Calculator" as of May 4, 2015, for someone born May 1, 1953, with earned income equal to or greater than the maximum Social Security wage base. No cost of living adjustment.

c) ***Withholding***: One sound reason to wait on your Social Security check is the "withholding" rule. This rule states that if you start taking your Social Security income early and report more than $18,240 (as of 2020) per year in earned income, then 50 percent of your Social Security check is taxed. Even though you may be receiving a higher payment when you turn your full retirement age based on these "withholdings," it does significantly impact the amount you receive.[5]

This $18,240 is based on earned income, not passive income. Passive income is income from pensions, interest, annuities or dividends. There are creative ways of getting our earned income below this $18,240 threshold.

For example, contributions to qualified accounts and gifting would be two ways to reduce your earned income under this baseline threshold. As we see it, if you are able to work, and you want to work, then your health is probably pretty good. This means that delaying your Social Security income payments will probably be in your best interest. The folks who really should be careful are the ones who decide to retire, take early payments, and then have to come out of retirement for one reason or another. Unless you are Brett Favre, coming in and out of retirement could have negative financial consequences. Favre, a famous footballer who played quarterback for the Green Bay Packers from 1992 to 2007, might just hold the record for retiring and un-retiring, having hung up his cleats in 2007, 2009, 2010 and, finally, in 2011. If you think you may want to continue working after reaching retirement age (age 62), you will definitely want to delay taking your Social Security payments until you make up your mind.

d) Spouse: The final factor to consider when deciding whether to take early payments has to do with your spouse. What is his or her Social Security situation? Is your spouse's benefit higher than yours? Will he/she have a higher benefit in the future? When one spouse passes away, the surviving spouse begins receiving the higher Social Security payment amount, not both.

For example, in a typical middle-income household, a couple is nearing retirement age. The husband is earning a Social

---

[5] Social Security Administration. 2019. "How Work Affects Your Benefits." https://www.ssa.gov/pubs/EN-05-10069.pdf

Security income of $2,000 per month. The wife's Social Security income is $1,000 per month. If either the husband or the wife dies, the $1,000 monthly income from the wife's Social Security will disappear, leaving the surviving spouse with the $2,000 per month. This plays an important role, because if your personal payments are scheduled to be the higher payment, then deferring these payments might be in your best interest. Not only are you increasing your own personal income base and the additional cost-of-living adjustment, but you are increasing the income base for your spouse, if you were to die before him or her.

On the flip side to aiming for the higher income, if you know your scheduled payments are going to be lower than those of your spouse, taking early payments is not unwise. Since your smaller payments are going away upon the death of either you or your spouse, it matters less if you decide to begin your Social Security income at age 62.

Another spousal option to consider is a ***Restricted Application for Spousal Benefits Only.*** This is the benefit where, once a spouse reaches their full retirement age (FRA), they have the ability to take half of their spouses FRA benefit. During this time, their own benefit still continues to grow until they are age 70, at which point they can stop taking spousal benefits and take their much higher age 70 benefit forever. Anyone that was at least age 62 or older by Dec. 31, 2015, is grandfathered into being able to do this. Remember, you can't do it until you reach your full retirement age, and only if you were at least age 62 by Dec. 31, 2015. [6]

All of this may seem confusing and a little morbid. No one wants to think about his or her own death or the death of a

---

[6] Social Security Administration. "Benefits Planner: Retirement." https://www.ssa.gov/planners/retire/claiming.html

spouse. But from a financial perspective, it is important to understand these nuances of Social Security that come with retirement planning.

According to Social Security's 2019 Annual Report, the trust fund will be depleted by 2035 by that is without any congressional actions, so we don't know exactly how long Social Security is going to be around.[7] We do know that we are paying into this fund that is supposed to help us when it is time for us to retire from our careers. For some of us, we may wonder: Will we ever see that money again? It depends on our current age and the government's ability to repair the cracks in the program's foundation.

For those of us who are nearing retirement age, however, the opportunity to benefit from Social Security is still pretty reliable, and there are several factors to consider when it comes to when we activate our Social Security benefits. Knowing how to trigger Social Security depends upon the assets you have saved up and when you plan on retiring. Everyone's situation is different. Avoid the tendency to follow the herd or take the advice of well-meaning friends or relatives. It is worth going to a financial advisor who can discuss your particular situation and utilize specially designed software to help you make a decision on how and when to file so you don't leave any money on the table. We can make this easy for you.

2. Income & Expense Analysis

The second, and one of the most important parts of any income plan, is your income and expense analysis. First, you analyze how much income you will have coming in from various sources such as Social Security or a pension. Then, with

---

[7] Social Security Administration. 2019. "A Summary of the 2019 Annual Reports." https://www.ssa.gov/oact/trsum/

the help of a qualified financial advisor, you forecast your retirement expenses. What do you want your lifestyle to be like? Where will you live? How much will you pay for household expenses? Will you want to travel? Will you spend extra money on grandkids? How much will health care cost? These expenses must all be factored in with after-tax income. We can't forget about the IRS and Uncle Sam! He is a major player. Twenty-five percent of your assets may be his. That's why tax planning is one of the key steps to our *Retirement Road Map®* process and which we'll discuss in a later chapter.

The key is to put together an itemized monthly budget, then compare it with your total income from your pension and/or Social Security to see if you'll be able to cover your monthly expenses. If not, we call that an income gap. Now, you will have an income goal to cover that gap or deficit which can be met by several financial planning strategies, one of which we'll explore later in this chapter. At SHP Financial, we provide you with the tools to make it easy for you to calculate and track your living expenses. Then, as a part of your plan, your advisor will provide you with various options for generating the needed income, as well as the benefits and drawbacks of each.

3. Inflation Plan

Once we know the amount of income you will need, we need to build your income plan in a way that will adjust for inflation. As we all know, the cost of a gallon of milk today is much higher than it was 20 years ago. The cost of the goods and services that we all need consistently increases.

The following chart shows the average annual inflation rate for each decade. Some decades saw from 5 to 9 percent average inflation per year! Can you imagine what that would do to your retirement nest egg? [8]

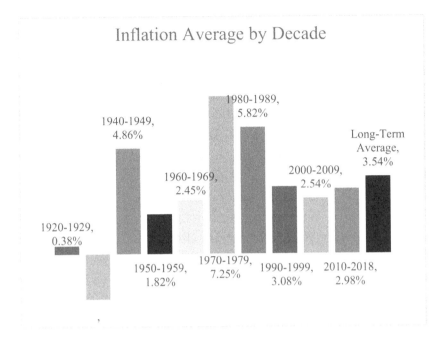

Since 1914, the long-term average inflation rate is 3.30 percent, which means it is more than likely prices will continue to rise over the years.[9] What is more interesting and frustrating is that inflation hits different ways. For example, rising at an even faster rate than general inflation are health care costs. The following chart shows the percentage increase in overall inflation as measured by the consumer price index (CPI) and health care inflation from 2008 through January 31, 2018.[10]

---

[8] InflationData.com. March 13, 2018. "Annual Inflation." https://inflationdata.com/Inflation/Inflation/AnnualInflation.asp

[9] US Inflation Calculator. Updated March 13, 2018. "Historical Inflation Rates: 1914-2018." http://www.usinflationcalculator.com/inflation/historical-inflation-rates/

[10] The FRED Blog. FRED Economic Data. "Healthy Inflation?: Inflation in the healthcare industry vs. general CPI." https://fredblog.stlouisfed.org/2017/07/healthy-inflation/

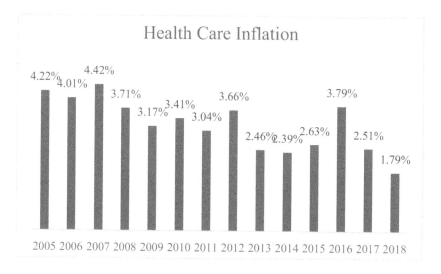

As you can see, U.S. health care inflation rose higher than the CPI in each year except 2008 and 2011. In most cases, the difference is quite significant. Preparing for such health care costs should be an overall part of your retirement plan, which is why it is one of five key areas of our *Retirement Road Map®* process that we will cover later.

You must consider how inflation will impact your retirement. Your income plan needs to reflect inflation and be prepared to deal with rising costs of goods and services. If you do not plan for inflation, you may put your retirement at risk. If your income does not keep up with the cost of living, it is more than likely that you will have to adjust the way you live later in your retirement years. That's why it is incredibly important to build an income plan that increases every year to account for inflation.

4. Spousal Plan

The fourth part of your income plan is what we call a spousal income plan. What happens to one spouse if the other passes away? Will the surviving spouse keep all of the pension, Social Security or other income coming in, or will there be a reduction?

Typically, you will automatically lose the lowest check upon death. How will the surviving spouse continue to cover his or her living expenses?

If you are married, we highly recommend that you take steps to ensure your income plan will carry over to your spouse. We're not talking about your account values, but rather, the income. Throughout the years in this business, we have seen so many retirees come in with a plan for income that does not account for a loss of income due to death or a change to their tax status as the widow(er) goes from "married filing jointly" to a "single filer." Additionally, we have seen many people who think that when their spouse passes away, the surviving spouse's income needs will be reduced — since the financial necessities will reduce from the needs of two people to that of one person. However, many times that is not the case, and the living spouse's income needs actually stay relatively the same.

A well-rounded retirement plan will take these questions into consideration and have strategies in place to ensure that the surviving spouse will continue to have the same quality of life without the fear of running out of money or not being able to pay his or her bills. How much more comfortable would you feel, knowing you have a plan in place to provide income for the rest of you *and* your spouse's lives?

The Evolution of the Income Plan

Thirty to 40 years ago, there were many companies that offered their long-term employees a defined benefit plan — a pension. Back then, the combination of pension, Social Security and your retirement assets made up the three legs of the "retirement stool."

Most people who have been lucky enough to have a pension are able to cover the majority of their annual expenses between their pension and their Social Security. In these cases, the third leg of the stool, retirement assets, are not as important and your lifestyle is not as affected by swings in the market.

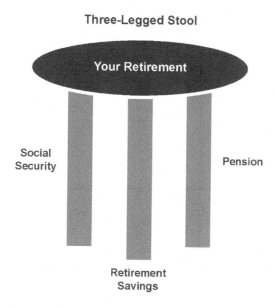

However, with the evolution of the 401(k), or defined contribution plan, in the early 1980s, many employers moved away from offering pensions and began offering defined contribution plans. With life expectancies rising, many companies decided they did not want to take the risk of giving their employees a check every month for the rest of their lives. Instead, they put the responsibilities for that check back on their employees' shoulders.

Defined contribution plans are things such as 401(k), 403(b) and other accounts that you, as the employee, contribute to, hopefully with an employer match. Basically, these accounts put the onus on employees to fund their own retirements. They also shift the investment risk to the employee. This has changed the three-legged stool into a two legged-stool, which, you can imagine, is not as stable.

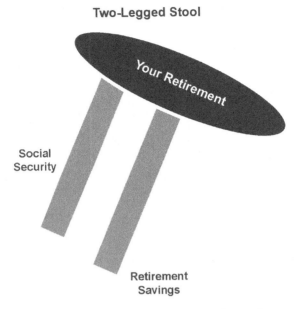

If you are someone with a two-legged stool — with only Social Security and your retirement assets to count on — it will become even more important to protect your assets and preserve them. They will need to last the rest of your life.

4 Percent Rule — Is It Still a Safe Withdrawal Rate?

The 4 Percent Rule is a rule of thumb that is used to determine the amount of funds to withdraw from a portfolio each year. The 4 Percent Rule was first articulated in 1994 by retired financial advisor William Bengen. Based upon his research of stock returns and retirement scenarios over a period of 75 years, he determined that retirees who drew down no more than 4.2 percent of their portfolio in the initial year of retirement and adjusted that amount each year thereafter for inflation stood a good chance of not outliving their money.

The goal was to provide a steady stream of funds to the retiree, while also keeping an account balance that would allow funds to be withdrawn for a number of years. This became traditionally thought of as a "safe" withdrawal rate, with adjustments for inflation as needed.

For example, if you had $500,000 for retirement, at age 65 you should be able to start taking a 4 percent withdrawal per year, or $20,000, and increase that amount by 3 percent per year for inflation. Theoretically, that rate of withdrawal and increases would allow you to live comfortably and have enough money to last the rest of your life. However, a number of studies in recent years looked into how this philosophy and other retirement income strategies stacked up.

Morningstar published a study in January 2013 indicating that, in a low bond yield environment such as the one we were in at that time,

> "a 4 percent initial withdrawal rate has approximately a 50 percent probability of success over a 30-year period [for a portfolio of 60 percent bonds/40 percent equities]. Would you want to flip a coin to determine your retirement income? For a retiree, at age 65, who wants a 90 percent probability of achieving a retirement income goal with a 30-year time horizon and a 40 percent equity portfolio would only have an initial withdrawal rate of 2.8 percent."[11]

Think about it. Think about how a 2.8 percent withdrawal rate would impact your life. If you have $1 million and you rely solely on the market to drive your income in retirement, would

---

[11] David Blanchett, Michael Finke, Wade D. Pfau. Morningstar. Jan. 21, 2013. "Low Bond Yields and Safe Portfolio Withdrawal Rates." https://corporate.morningstar.com/us/documents/targetmaturity/LowBondYieldsWithdrawalRates.pdf.

you be able to live off of $28,000 per year? Since bond rates and Federal Reserve actions are unpredictable, we don't have a crystal ball to be able to see when we might once again face a prolonged period of low interest rates.

One factor that impacts the revised withdrawal rate is due to what the article refers to as "return sequence risk." Simply put, this means that, once withdrawals are being made, the timing of losses can negatively impact the longevity of a portfolio. This is especially if that timing is at or near retirement. A nice catchy term for this is "reverse dollar-cost averaging."

Going backward is huge when you are no longer contributing to an account. Instead, you are depleting the account little by little to replace your paycheck. When you were younger and were still in the accumulation state of your life, if you were making regular, systematic contributions into an investment portfolio, you actually benefited from the ups and downs of the market. It is a rule of investing known as "dollar-cost averaging."[12]

Here's the way it worked when you were in the accumulation phase: If the stock market was up, that was great. Your account balance was up, too. If the stock market was down, that was OK, too. Why? Because you were making regular contributions to an account that bought shares with each deposit you made. The shares were cheaper when the market was down. The key was to keep making those regular contributions to the account. With time on your side, you were able to smooth out the volatility no matter which way the market moved.

What helped you in the accumulation stage could now hurt you as you transition to retirement. Think about it. If you stop contributing to the account on a regular basis and now begin

---

[12] Dollar-cost averaging does not assure a profit or protect against loss in declining markets.

withdrawing on a regular basis, you are now selling shares out of your account, not buying them. So, if you take out 4 percent and the market loses 4 percent, you just withdrew, in essence, 8 percent, didn't you? Your bills don't stop coming in, and your expenses can't be put on hold. It's not like you get a call from your mortgage company and they say, "Hey, we heard the market is down so you don't have to pay your mortgage this month!" Wouldn't that be nice? Instead, you have to sell more shares to keep the income coming in. What was that sound? It was you just getting run over by reverse dollar-cost averaging.

If you are consistently withdrawing 4 percent from an equity-based account, you have to factor in market losses as being tacked onto your withdrawals.

So, what was a normal 5 percent loss became 9 percent once you factored in your 4 percent withdrawal. What was a 10 percent loss now becomes 14 percent. While you have your slide ruler out, calculate this: In a losing scenario, folks would have to earn 12 percent to overcome a loss of 9 percent.

Consider this statement from William Sharpe, a 1990 Nobel Prize winning economist:

> "Supporting a constant spending plan using a volatile investment policy is fundamentally flawed. A retiree using a 4 Percent Rule faces spending shortfalls when risky investments underperform, may accumulate wasted surpluses when they outperform, and, in any case, could likely purchase exactly the same spending distributions more cheaply."[13]

In other words, if our "at-risk" funds underperform, we are in big trouble with the 4 Percent Rule.

---

[13] Jason S. Scott, William F. Sharpe and John G. Watson. 2009. "The 4% Rule—At What Price?" Journal of Investment Management, Vol. 7, No. 3. Page 31-48.

Annuities: To Buy or Not to Buy?

When we're building an income plan for our clients, as the first step to our *Retirement Road Map®* process, one of the first questions we ask them is if they want their retirement income guaranteed or not guaranteed.

Security Benefit Life Insurance Company did a study about planning for certainty in retirement. They hired Milliman Inc., an independent actuarial firm, to study outcomes of popular retirement income generation strategies. They looked at a hypothetical scenario comparing the success of a market-based portfolio to a financial strategy with a significant portion (up to 60 percent) of a portfolio allocated to a fixed index annuity contract with an income rider, both strategies equal to a starting value of $1 million and both anticipating annual withdrawals of up to 4.5 percent. In this comparison, the strategy using only market-based instruments (largely mutual funds) had at most an 82 percent probability of success. Not too shabby, but who wants to be in the remaining 18 percent? The strategy that included mutual funds but was anchored in a fixed index annuity, however, had a 99.5 percent probability of success. [14]

This study points to the potential value of adding annuities to an income strategy. An annuity can be a great addition to your retirement plan, providing income month after month for the rest of your life that rises with inflation. However, while there are over 100 annuities in the marketplace, there are only a handful that we would recommend. As fiduciary advisors, at SHP Financial we would only recommend a particular annuity if it was the best option for you in your situation. Since annuities' guarantees are only as strong as the claims-paying ability of

---

[14] Security Benefit. March 2017. "Planning with Certainty: A New Strategy for Retirement Income." http://austinfirstfinancial.com/wp-content/uploads/2017/03/Planning-with-certainty.pdf.

their issuing carriers, the financial strength of the carrier is one factor to consider when determining what annuity might fit in your financial picture.

In our opinion, there are some types of annuities that you should stay clear from. Yet, there are some fixed index annuities that we would highly recommend to a client if their goal was to have their income guaranteed by an insurance company. There are other ways to guarantee your income, but it's all about making sure your assets are diversified properly. To buy or not to buy depends upon the balance you desire between guarantees versus flexibility. It also depends upon your desire for growth versus stability. There are no easy answers, but how you feel about these issues goes a long way to determine if an annuity would be a good fit for you.

The bottom line is that every person's circumstance is different, and we highly recommend you meet with a qualified financial advisor before making any decisions on setting up an income plan.

Lessons From 2008

It's important to remember our history, so we don't repeat the same mistakes. It is not hard to forget such a scary time economically when the subsequent years—while full of political drama—saw markets on the longest bull run in American history. For many, this long market run led to complacency about market risk. Although the country lived through and recovered from the market crash of 2008, there are important lessons that should not be forgotten.

Let's say, hypothetically, in 2008 you deposited $500,000 in a retirement account tied to the S&P 500. In the first year, you would have lost about 39 percent of your money. Now you are down to only $307,000. After a few years, the market did recover. It gained 49 percent, in fact. But at that rate, you still would not have made back your principal even if you were not taking withdrawals at the time.

For those who still had a long time before they were going to retire, eventually they would have made all of their money back. For this example, however, let's say you were in or near retirement at that time and needed to withdraw 5 percent per year, or $25,000 from your portfolio. It is 2008, you're happy because you've just retired with $500,000 in your account, and you are withdrawing 5 percent per year to cover your expense. Suddenly, the market crashes. In this case, because you are drawing down $25,000 per year, your account has been reduced to $282,000. Your withdrawal rate just went from 5 percent to almost 10 percent in one year! If you are retired, and you need to take those withdrawals, you don't have time to wait for the market to recover. Your bills are going to keep coming in and you need to continue taking withdrawals from your account. In most cases, you're in danger of running out of money.

That scenario was a reality. We saw this firsthand. People would come to our office in a panic saying that their previous broker did not set them up properly. A loss early on in retirement can be devastating if your accounts are not set up the right way.

Let us be clear: We have nothing against the market. A large portion of our business is managing our clients' money in the market through strategic and institutional management — something we will get into in the next chapter. Furthermore, these crashes are all natural and inherent to the market and capitalism itself. It is healthy for these corrections to exist, but it's not good for retirees who are relying on those assets for their paychecks. A downturn at the wrong time is what we are trying to prevent, especially with the assets that are earmarked for income.

The bottom line is that you must be really careful when and how you are withdrawing money in retirement from market funds. At SHP Financial, we believe it's important to have a plan for a solid foundation of reliable, predictable income before you risk too much of your assets in the stock market, thereby reducing the stress of wondering whether or not another 2008 will harm your future retirement plans. For example, what will the 2020s be like? Will they be like the 1990s and 2010s? Or will the market look more like the 2000s? No one knows. That uncertainty is not something we like to see in the foundation of retirement: your income plan.

Conclusion: Retirement Is Not the Time to Gamble

The biggest key to your income plan is to realize that this is not the time to be gambling. Income-producing assets should dominate the financial vehicles you will rely on in retirement. Conversely, assets with the possibility to reduce income should not be among the financial vehicles you depend on for income — although there is a place for these assets within your overall retirement plan. Even in today's environment, it may be possible to achieve predictable and steady cash flow with a customized income strategy.

We believe the best strategy is to have three lanes with a purpose and goal to each. Typically, in lane one, we have some assets designated for ***income***. In lane two, we have some for ***safety*** (in case of an emergency) and in lane three we have some used for ***growth***. Once you know that you have a stable income covering your basic expenses, you can relax and allow your investment assets to grow without worrying about how market fluctuations will affect your retirement.

Let's take a look at an example of clients who recently came to us. This couple wanted to retire in five years and had $1.3 million in retirement savings. Their combined Social Security benefits came to $3,000 per month. Neither the husband nor the wife had a pension. The income and expense analysis we did for them showed they would need at least $6,000 per month to cover their living expenses. That left them with a $3,000 monthly gap or deficit that needed to be covered year after year, with inflation. How would you do that?

In this case, we segregated a portion of their assets (about $700,000) for their income plan using a combination of vehicles — some vehicles guaranteed by insurance companies, some market-based like bonds and dividend-paying stocks — that would generate $3,000 per month of income coming in month after month, year after year, and that would also increase over time for inflation. This strategy gave them confidence that they had a stable income to cover their expenses for the rest of their lives. We also moved a portion of their assets ($100,000) to a vehicle that offered safety and liquidity, where they could have assets available for an emergency. Finally, we took their remaining $500,000 in assets and directed them into their investment plan, with the goal of growing and protecting those assets for the future and/or to leave to their heirs.

When we talk about the five-step *Retirement Road Map®* plan we create for folks, an income plan is the first and most important step we address, because it's the foundation of your retirement. If you are lucky enough to have one or more pensions coming in when you retire, and that plus your Social Security is enough to cover your expenses, then your income plan may already be in really good shape. However, with pensions becoming obsolete, many of you will need a customized income plan to transition you from saving money during your working years to turning that money into retirement income to pay for the lifestyle you want and deserve in your retirement years. You've worked hard and sacrificed all of your working years, and now it's time to have the retirement you have always dreamed of.

Don't spend your golden years worrying about running out of money. If you're at or near retirement, it's critical to get help from a qualified professional financial advisor to create a customized, written retirement plan to generate income to cover your expenses year after year, including inflation, for the rest of your life.

CHAPTER TWO

Investment Planning

Once you have your income plan — the cornerstone of your retirement plan — in place, then it is important to decide how you want your remaining money invested. This is established within your investment plan — the second step of our *Retirement Road Map®* process. By establishing a solid income plan first, you can afford to be a bit more aggressive with the rest of your assets (if you choose to be), because you already know you will have reliable income payments through your withdrawal plan. The primary step to establishing your investment plan is to hire a financial advisory team of fiduciaries who are bound by law to always do what is in your best interest, and whose sole job is to create, implement and manage your entire portfolio in a comprehensive and structured way.

Then you move onto the age old question of risk vs reward. How much risk are you willing to take at this stage in your life? Is it worth the reward? One motto that we live by is from the Oracle of Omaha, Mr. Warren Buffett who said, "why risk what you have for something you don't need?[15]" After your income plan is established and you are working with a fiduciary, let's turn to this question.

Misunderstanding Risk

There are two main components of risk: risk tolerance and risk capacity.

1. Risk Tolerance

Most of the clients who come into our offices have heard of this term but it is important to decide what your current risk tolerance is and to understand the current risk in your retirement portfolio. Risk tolerance itself is an emotional and visceral feeling that needs to be measured against what you own. How much risk can you physically tolerate? When does it stop being fun? How much risk is too much? When your health is affected and the stress isn't worth it. It's of utmost importance to make sure that your portfolio matches up with your risk tolerance.

Risk tolerance, like taste, should change over time. Do you still like the same foods or the same wines as you did when you were 21 years old? Probably not. The same goes for your risk tolerance. Why, then, should your investments stay the same as you age and approach retirement?

2. Risk Capacity

Where risk tolerance is physical, risk capacity is financial. This is strictly based on cash flow or disposable income. If all your income is going toward bills and debts, you don't have the capacity to risk anything. If your net income is sufficient to

---

[15] CNBC Interview. February 26, 2018. "Unofficial transcript."
https://www.cnbc.com/2018/02/26/full-transcript-billionaire-investor-warren-buffett-speaks-with-cnbcs-becky-quick-on-squawk-box-today.html

cover your lifestyle, then you are free to move some assets into investments. If not, then no matter how aggressive you are, there is not much capacity to invest.

Over the years, we have had many people come into our office from our radio show, various workshops and many client referrals. Typically, when we meet with them they tell us how conservative they would like to be with their assets. They explain to us how they were initially set up with a conservative portfolio but it hasn't been rebalanced in years. Then, more often than not, we end up finding out that the risk they think they have and are comfortable with is not what is actually reflected in their accounts. What's worse is that we see a lot of target date funds, the types of mutual funds that are tied to a specific age of retirement have much more downside risk than is apparent.

One of the first things we do when a potential client comes to us is run a risk analysis on their portfolio. Through *Morningstar*™ and *Riskalyze*™ or other third-party analysis, we're able to look at their portfolio in a number of different scenarios. For example, if there was another 2008, or a similar economic crisis, we can relatively gauge what could happen in their portfolio. Many times, our clients are surprised to find their portfolios are subject to much more risk than they thought or are actually comfortable with.

For example, we had a couple, Bob and Denise, come into our office and ask for help in setting up a *Retirement Road Map*®. As we dove into their investment plan, they told us that, about three years earlier, as they were getting closer to retirement age, they asked their broker to adjust their portfolio to make it more conservative. They felt they had saved a good chunk of retirement savings at this point in their lives, and they wanted to protect it.

As we do with all of our clients, we ran a risk analysis on Bob and Denise's portfolio. What we found was that their portfolio was not nearly as conservative as they would have liked. In fact, the way their portfolio was set up, they could stand to lose close to 42 percent if another market crash happened. That's almost half of their entire lives' savings. It happened in 1987, in 2001 and again in 2008. In 2019 the market began the year with some stumbles before continuing its climb to all time heights and to the longest bull market in stock market history but…o one knows when the next stumble will turn into a major market correction. Market bubbles, crashes and corrections are a good thing for our economy in the long term, but are not for our retirees.

Often we wonder what the next decade will look like. Will it look like the 2010's and the bull market with no end? Or will it be like the 2000's which many call the "lost decade?" If you are at or near retirement you can't afford to be unprepared. That's why, when developing your investment plan, it's important to diversify your assets. For example, you can diversify your investment plan by setting aside a chunk for emergency funds, a chunk for income, and a chunk for growth or you can use the bucket theory of having certain accounts invested in such a way so that they are withdrawn in certain time periods with an investment mix to match.. If you desire to have an investment plan that has some risk for growth, it's important to make sure that you have the proper income plan built first. If you are not confident that your current investments and asset allocations are balanced to afford you reliable retirement income and long-term growth, see a qualified financial advisor to get a second opinion on your portfolio and set up a comprehensive investment plan.

Which Vehicle to Use?

Caution: High Fees Ahead

Most often when a client first comes to our office they have mutual funds (a.k.a. retail investments) that are loaded with high, hidden fees and tax inefficiencies. They have no idea how much in fees they are actually paying because the fees are buried deep in their portfolios with zero transparency. There are unexpected trade fees, loads and 12b-1 fees — which are marketing fees passed on to you as the investor. Basically, you are paying a higher cost to own a "pool" of stocks and/or bonds.

This point is illustrated in an article published by Barron's, entitled, "The Hidden Costs of Doing Business."[16] In the article, the author discusses a study performed by Roger Edelen, a finance professor at the University of California Davis. This study revealed that, in the nearly 1800 mutual funds that Edelen and his co-authors looked at, they had an average expense ratio of 1.19 percent when you looked at the prospectus. But, when looking deeper revealed another 1.44 percent in trading costs on average. As a result the average cost of these funds is not the 1.19 percent that the fund owners see. It's really the 1.19 plus the 1.44 for a total average cost of 2.63 percent. According to Edelen, "investors think they know their funds' expenses, but they're really only seeing half the picture."

Most clients will come in telling us they're only paying 1 percent to their broker, but after doing a fee analysis on their portfolio we often uncover invisible costs such as transaction fees that are eating away at their returns. In some cases, clients are really paying closer to 2.5 percent and they don't even know

---

[16] Beverly Goodman. Barron's. March 2, 2013. "The Hidden Cost of Doing Business."
http://www.barrons.com/articles/SB50001424052748704356104578326293404837234.

it. If you have a $500,000 portfolio you may think you are paying $5,000 a year in fees, but you actually may be paying close to $12,500 per year. Imagine what else you could have done with that $12,500, such as traveling, home improvements or investing in your grandchildren's college education. The possibilities are endless.

Capital Gains Costs on Post-Tax Accounts

Mutual funds have a number of tax inefficiencies. Among them are this vehicle's capital gains taxes. Capital gains are when a mutual fund has assets that have grown over time and sells them during the current tax year. At tax time, all of the investors will have to pay capital gains taxes. This is true whether you are an investor who has held shares in the mutual fund for several years, or you are a new investor who bought the mutual fund's shares at the very end of the year and whose assets didn't actually see any growth. There are two types of capital gains taxes: short-term and long-term.

Long-term capital gains taxes apply to any assets the mutual fund held for a year or more. These are taxed at a standard 15 percent rate. Short-term capital gains taxes apply to assets the fund bought and sold within a year, and are taxed according to your income tax bracket.

Additionally, when capital gains are assessed, mutual funds readjust share prices. This means that, even if you reinvest the gains your shares made, your total investment hasn't changed — even though the value of your shares did. If you have invested in the mutual fund for less than a year, you may still have to pay capital gains taxes even if your personal investment didn't increase at all. If you are a new investor, even if you lost money on your mutual fund holdings, as long as the mutual fund itself (and the other investors in it) made money during the course of the year, you may still have to pay capital gains tax.

Let's see how this plays out. Assume you are a new investor who bought 10 shares of a mutual fund at $10 each and then are assessed a short-term capital gain from the mutual fund's previous earnings:

Mutual Fund Gains		
Starting value	$100	10 x $10
Capital gain	$20	$2 per share
New share price	$8	$10 minus the $2 capital gain distribution to shareholders
Capital gain reinvested	$20 ÷ $8 per share	2.5 shares purchased
Ending value	$100	$12.5 x $8

The value of your assets hasn't changed, but you still have a tax liability. The $20 short-term capital gain that built up over the course of the year might be taxed at 25 percent, depending on your income tax rate. As a result, if you pay $5 in taxes, your account will actually be $95 when all is said and done.

If you "unwrapped" the mutual fund and owned the stock of the companies contained therein or explored a more tax efficient exchange traded fund ("ETF"), you would be able to defer taxes on your gains. But, as a mutual fund shareholder, you have to pay those taxes annually even if you reinvested all of your gains.

At SHP Financial, as fiduciary advisors, when we manage our clients' investments, we use the institutional investment model. The name is derived by the style of investing that large companies or "institutions" utilize. For example, if an institution has a billion dollars to invest, do you think the advisor would have that money in retail market funds? Definitely not. The institution would demand transparency, the lowest expense ratio, and no loads. For these and many other reasons, we choose to offer institutional investing. We want to be more transparent and reduce our clients' fees. Also, there are no trading commissions in this model, which is very important to us as fiduciary advisors. We have always found it strange for an advisor to get paid a commission for placing a trade. From the perspective of the client, it brings into question whether the advisor made a trade because it was in the client's best interest, or if the trade was affected just to make the advisor more money in fees.

To us, institutional investing is the only way that makes sense. In the institutional world, you are buying individual stocks, bonds, ETF's or a no-load, low expense ratio mutual fund) instead of buying a front loaded retail mutual fund with all of the hidden fees in it. Dealing with a fiduciary that embraces institutional investing provides the comfort to know that you are on the same side of the table and share the same goals as your advisor. No one wants to pay unnecessary fees and everyone should know exactly what they are paying for their advice. This is what you receive from a fiduciary with institutional money management: full transparency and an alignment of goals.

Active vs. Strategic Money Management

As a part of our investment plan and institutional investment model, you have the options of what we call "active" or "strategic" money management. We use both models for our clients at SHP Financial.

Strategic, or passive, management has been proven to work time as active managers have difficulty in beating their benchmark on a consistent basis. Strategic management means buying different index funds or low-cost ETFs and owning almost the whole market at a cost-efficient price. The goal is to remain in the market through thick and thin but in a strategic way. For example, the portfolios would be rebalanced on a semi-annual basis, audited to ensure you have the "best in breed" of the funds, and tilted to take advantage of long term trends. This method may work long-term, but when you go through those big drops in the market, you really feel it and need to be prepared for it.

By contrast, with an actively managed portfolio, the managers have more freedom. The money managers we work with who are in the active (or tactical) space are not limited. Some have the ability to quickly go to cash and make changes to either reduce risk or increase return. At SHP Financial, we provide our clients with the option to access to a team of institutional money managers for active management that they otherwise would not have access to unless they had a certain minimum level of assets, usually from $1 million to $5 million or more.

We also have actively managed portfolios that are always "hedged." This means they are managed in a way that attempts to only have up to a minimum amount they can lose. On the upside, it performs almost as well but usually not quite as much as the overall market. This is a strategy that many clients really appreciate, especially as they are in their retirement years.

CHAPTER THREE

Tax Planning

Tax efficiency is a big piece of the retirement puzzle. That's why tax planning is the third step in our *Retirement Road Map®* planning process and one we leverage on behalf of our clients as much as possible. Unlike Investment and Income planning where things can change based on the markets or budgets, tax planning is based on concrete knowledge of the tax code. In other words, we don't have to speculate when it comes to taxes. When Congress acts, we act because it is now the law of the land and if your advisor isn't making sure that the tax code is working for you, it might well be working against you. If you're like most people, you probably see your tax professional once per year at tax time to file your annual return. At your annual meeting, how much proactive tax planning occurs for the upcoming year? Probably not much at all. That's tax *preparing*, not tax *planning*. In fact, some CPAs see their job as lowering your taxes as much as possible in that given year as compared to looking at what potential tax brackets could be. Again, they are focused on tax preparing as compared to tax planning.

Tax planning is where a tax or qualified financial professional looks at your current situation to help you identify potential areas where you may have unnecessary tax liabilities, or whereupon a future event you may experience an undesirable tax consequence. The goal is to see what can be done proactively throughout the year, if anything, to reduce your future tax liabilities. These are things we not only address initially as we bring on a new client, but they are also something we re-assess each year during semi-annual or annual client reviews.

Are Taxes on the Rise?

Are we likely to significantly reduce our national spending? It's doubtful. Can this have implications for taxes in the future? Absolutely. With the Tax Cuts and Jobs Act of 2017, tax brackets were set quite low. Yet, barring an act of Congress, the new brackets are set to sunset back to previous levels after 2025. Given this plus the current amount of national debt and spending, it is a likely conclusion that during your retirement, tax rates will increase. Bottom line, taxes are on sale, and the key is to figure out how you can take advantage of it.

Have you considered how a tax rate increase could impact your retirement accounts? These accounts very likely represent your biggest potential tax liability, especially if your largest account is an individual retirement account (IRA) or 401(k). Why? Every dollar that comes out is taxable. Think of it as having a partner in your business of retirement. His name is Uncle Sam, and you owe him a portion of your net worth. Generally speaking, the income from your retirement account is taxable at whatever your highest income rate is. Additionally, there is also the possibility that, as you withdraw money out of your IRA, it can increase the amount of Social Security income that is taxable.

As an example, say you've reached age 72, and the IRS will now require you to take required minimum distributions (RMDs) from your IRAs, SEP IRAs, Simple IRAs, etc. If your RMD is $50,000 a year in withdrawals out of your IRAs and you are in a 25 percent tax bracket, you'll be paying $12,500 in taxes. Now, let's say you still have quite a few years left before you need to withdraw that money. We just determined that the tax rates are likely going to rise, right? So, what if in 10 to 15 years your tax rate is 40 percent? Then you'll be paying $20,000 a year in taxes. This is a huge pitfall, and something that can be hedged or avoided all together if planning is done ahead of time.

Tax Planning Strategies to Buy Out Uncle Sam

Roth IRA Conversions

One way to reduce future taxes on your IRA would be to convert your account to a Roth IRA. Roth IRAs have the benefit of tax-free growth as well as tax-free withdrawals for you and your beneficiaries. That is because the money you contribute to a Roth IRA has already been taxed.

Distributions from a Roth IRA are tax free and penalty free as long as the five-year aging period is met and the account owner is 59 ½ years of age or older, disabled or deceased. At SHP Financial, our advisors stay up to date on the latest Roth IRA conversion rules and can sit down with you to discuss whether or not converting your traditional IRA or 401(k) to a Roth IRA might be a good choice for you. (We might also consider a partial conversion).

Although the IRS has defined income restrictions for who may contribute to a Roth IRA, anyone may convert the assets of an existing IRA to a Roth IRA. However, it is important to decide whether or not converting to a Roth IRA is the right option for you.

If you decide to convert your current IRA's assets to a Roth IRA, you will have to pay federal income taxes on the total amount you convert, and at your regular income tax rate. You'll want to make sure that you are always aware of what tax bracket you will be in so that you don't convert too much all at once and bump yourself into a higher tax bracket. Many times, we have found the best strategy is to convert small portions of your accounts to Roth IRAs over time.

Consulting with a tax advisor is something you will want to consider prior to converting to a Roth IRA. At SHP Financial, we have certified public accountants (CPAs) who we work with to assist our clients with these issues. It is not always a perfect scenario. For example, if your tax bracket decreases during retirement, you may end up paying more in taxes with a conversion during a higher tax bracket year. However, you will have the benefits of the tax-free growth and withdrawals on those future earnings. And unlike traditional IRAs, there are no RMDs for Roth IRAs during the lifetime of the account owner.

More into Post-Tax Dollars

Whether the end result is a Roth Conversion or this strategy, the original step is the same. Withdrawing funds from the IRA assets at the most tax efficient time and then reinvesting the proceeds accordingly. The only difference is rather than flipping the proceeds into a Roth IRA, you would reinvest the funds into an after-tax brokerage account. Although you do not have the tax-free growth that a Roth IRA would provide, the brokerage account does allow for more flexibility when it comes to gifting the assets to the next generation or depositing into a 529 for college expenses.

Tax Loss Harvesting

As a part of your overall tax plan, it's important to look at all possible areas where you may be able to save your hard-earned dollars. One thing we can do for clients to reduce their tax burden is tax loss harvesting. Very few advisors are talking to their clients about this, and if you currently own mutual funds, you may not be able to do this as efficiently.

Let's say you have realized a decent amount of gains in a given year and you want to reduce them to reduce the amount of capital gains tax you will have to pay. Tax loss harvesting is when, at the end of the year, you sell all, or a portion of, your losing equities, then buy them back 31 days later if you want to. By realizing, or "harvesting" a loss, you are able to offset taxes on both gains and income, thereby reducing your overall tax burden.

There are some downsides to this scenario. For example, you must wait 31 days to buy the stocks back. This is the wash-sale rule imposed by the IRS (IRS Publication 550).[17] This prevents investors from repurchasing the security within 30 days before or after the sale. If you left it in cash, you may miss some of the market upside (or avoid some downside). In most cases, while waiting the 30-day period, you would replace that stock with a corresponding security, and there is always the chance that the new stock could increase your gains, should that stock rise in the 30-day period.

Additionally, there are some who think that long-term tax harvesting could inadvertently drive up your future tax rate. The bottom line is that you must consider your whole tax picture. You must consult a qualified financial advisor or tax accountant to discuss your particular situation to see if tax loss harvesting is

---

[17] IRS. Updated March 14, 2018. "Publication 550, Investment Income and Expenses." https://www.irs.gov/forms-pubs/about-publication-550

right for you. At SHP Financial, this is something we review at year-end with our clients to determine if this strategy makes sense.

SECURE Act of 2019

Late in December of 2019, the United States Congress passed one of the more sweeping laws that affect retirement and tax planning. Without going into all of the details of the legislation we wanted to provide the brief highlights:

1.) Age 72
   a. Raised the age of Required Minimum Distributions ("RMD's") to age 72. Originally, the year 70 ½ was in everyone's mind as when distributions must begin but now that confusing half year rule has been replaced with a flat age of 72.
   b. We were most excited about this change as it allows for more time for tax planning strategies to be utilized
2.) IRA Contributions
   a. If you are working and have earned income, you can continue to contribute to an IRA. What's comical about this change is that you can contribute and be forced to withdraw in the same year but that's the US Congress for you
3.) Inherited IRA's
   a. If you are a non-spouse and inherit an IRA, you will now have a maximum of 10 years to take the funds out. This is the biggest negative with the SECURE Act as the law lowers the limit from lifetime withdrawals to 10 years at most. This is yet another reason to actively tax plan and unwind

your pre-tax dollars into ROTH IRA's, after-tax funds, gifting, or leveraging life insurance (see below)

Although Congress moves slow, when changes do happen they have serious consequences. In order to have a complete financial plan, you need to be fully up to date with these changes and what they mean to you. That is why our Retirement Roadmap® incorporates tax planning to inform our clients of these events and make sure that the changes are working for them and not against them.

What to Do With Excess RMDs

One important question that comes up quite often is what to do with excess RMDs. As we've discussed, upon reaching 72 years of age, you will be required to take annual minimum distributions from your IRA or company retirement plans. These required distributions are included in your taxable income. If you don't need that entire distribution amount to cover expenses, there are several ways to reinvest that money.

1. Taxable Brokerage Accounts

You could consider moving funds to a taxable brokerage account, but keep in mind that you want to steer clear of securities that will generate excessive income or too-high short-term capital gain, thereby increasing your income taxes. Rather, focus on those investments that are tax efficient on a year-to-year basis.

2. Converting RMDs to Tax-Free Legacy

Converting excess RMDs to life insurance, a.k.a. a tax-free legacy, is another more tax-efficient option. If you leverage a portion of the RMD to purchase life insurance in an irrevocable life insurance trust (ILIT), the insurance proceeds will pass to your beneficiaries free of estate taxes. Combined with the income-tax-free death benefit that life insurance provides, this may be an excellent way to transfer excess RMDs to your heirs, tax free.

3. Postpone RMDs With a QLAC

Another option to reduce the amount of RMDs is to take a portion of your IRA portfolio and purchase a qualified longevity annuity contract (QLAC). A QLAC is a new breed of longevity annuity (also known as a deferred-income annuity). You set up a QLAC by transferring money from any of your existing IRA or 401(k) accounts to a special type of insurance company annuity. Your QLAC is designed to pay you a steady monthly income later in life (to protect against living too long).

According to regulations issued by the U.S. Treasury, you can put up to 25 percent (or not more than $135,000 for 2020, whichever is less) of your portfolio toward a QLAC. When you add the QLAC, it is deemed to count toward your RMDs. With a QLAC, you're not forced to withdraw an RMD at age 72, nor in any of the subsequent thirteen years. The tax savings from not having to withdraw RMDs for thirteen years will be significant. It also guarantees an income stream later in life.

4. Gifting & Charity

Gifting to your children, contributing to a Roth IRA on behalf of your child or grandchild, or gifting to a charity are other options for the RMDs themselves or excess RMDs. For example, the tax code allows for Qualified Charitable Contributions ("QCDs") which are gifts of up to $100,000 per person per year to qualifying charities that can go towards their RMD's for that year. Or retirees can steer their RMDs to certain charities, and, in doing so, the donated amount is eliminated from their adjusted gross income at tax time.

Leveraging Life Insurance

The IRS allows for life insurance to receive certain tax advantages that make it truly unique and one of the best legacy saving plans. Life insurance has some of the best, if not the best, tax advantages of any asset class. If structured properly, life insurance can offer an income-tax-free death benefit paid to your beneficiaries, the potential for tax-deferred cash accumulation, and income-tax-free loans and withdrawals, which can be used for tax-free income in retirement. There are no contribution limits based on income.

Let us digress here for a moment. We have many clients who earn too much money to contribute to a Roth IRA and who have maxed out their 401(k)s. For these folks, funding a life insurance policy can often produce similar tax advantages.

Additionally, there are no additional federal taxes or penalties for accessing your policy's cash value prior to age 59 ½ if it is not classified as a modified endowment contract. Some life insurance policies even offer income-tax-free benefits to help pay for the costs associated with long-term care or chronic illness. If we are using this method with tax-free future income or withdrawals, we are not looking to get the maximum death benefit. Rather, we are designing the policy more for cash access or accumulation.

Given these advantages, life insurance may be something to consider in your overall retirement strategy, complementing your fixed income assets and helping to manage and potentially reduce your total tax liability, as well as helping provide for your loved ones.

Also, some of our clients who want to leave a legacy may purchase a large life insurance policy. By doing so, it gives them the confidence to spend down their assets during their lifetime, knowing that they have a large, income-tax-free death benefit set aside for their heirs, even if they spend all of their money.

Tax Considerations for a Surviving Spouse

What if one spouse dies? In many cases, the surviving spouse's taxes could potentially increase. This can happen for many reasons. First, the year of death is the last year for which you can file your taxes jointly with your deceased spouse (unless you have a dependent child, see IRS Publication 501). Following that year, the surviving spouse becomes a single taxpayer, so his or her tax rate may increase due to becoming a single filer. Additionally, the surviving spouse will now only have one personal exemption and one standard deduction.

Second, in terms of Social Security benefits, the income thresholds for single people are different from those who are married, which can mean that a percentage of your benefits may now become taxable.

Third, to make up for the reduction in Social Security benefits upon death, the surviving spouse is often likely to take additional funds from an IRA. Because the IRA distributions are taxable, this has the potential to significantly increase the surviving spouse's income tax liability which is sometimes referred to as the "spousal income trap."

To address these issues, the first order of business would be to find out if you even have a potential problem. When we sit down with our clients, we do an analysis of what your circumstances would look like from a tax perspective if one of the spouses was no longer here.

If the results of that analysis show there is a potential problem, there are many different options that can be used to decrease this tax burden, including converting any IRA you have over to a nontaxable Roth, disclaiming a portion of the IRA at inheritance which means one accepting some of the IRA and giving the rest to your beneficiaries or putting your assets into a trust (which we will cover in Chapter Five). We suggest working with a financial advisor and tax professional team to develop a plan to address potential tax liabilities while meeting your needs.

Conclusion: Take a Team Approach

At SHP Financial, we include tax planning in our five-step *Retirement Road Map®* process because it's a critical part of your overall retirement plan. As a part of that plan, we perform a thorough review of your tax situation to see if there are areas that can be addressed to reduce the amount of money that is open to taxation by our federal and state governments. Then we review it again each year at our semi-annual or annual client reviews. After years in the industry, we have extensive knowledge in this area; however, we do not claim to be CPAs. We always recommend that you seek the advice of a qualified tax professional.

No one company can specialize in all things, but it's important for you to have a team approach when putting together your retirement plan. At SHP Financial, we can offer you a full team of professionals who will work together to create your customized *Retirement Road Map®* plan, and that includes CPAs who can consult and offer professional advice on the tax planning portion of your *Retirement Road Map®* plan.

CHAPTER FOUR

Health Care Planning

According to the latest retiree health care cost estimate from Fidelity's Benefits Consulting, a 65-year-old couple retiring this year will need an average of $275,000[18] (in today's dollars) to cover medical expenses throughout retirement. This does not even include the costs of long-term care.

That's basically a mortgage. Most people strive to pay their mortgage off before they retire so they won't have this large monthly payment weighing down their expenses. What about their health care costs? Many people we have seen over the years had not thought about how much health care would cost. They certainly didn't think it could be as much as their mortgage.

---

[18] Fidelity Investments. September 6, 2017. "Retiree health care costs continue to surge." https://www.fidelity.com/viewpoints/retirement/retiree-health-costs-rise

Managing the Costs of Health Care Before Age 65

Health care is one of the most, if not the most, costly expenses you'll face in retirement. Prior to age 65, if you are not getting health care coverage from your employer, insurance costs can range anywhere from $500 to $2,000 per month for an individual or couple. One of the best ways to help offset these costs if you are still working is to look into a health savings account, or HSA.

An HSA has characteristics of both traditional and Roth IRAs but are reserved for the express purpose of medical expenses. Funds contributed to this account are not subject to federal income taxes at the time of deposit. The funds can be withdrawn, tax free, from the account as long as they are used for qualified medical expenses, such as deductibles, co-pays and co-insurance. With a health savings account, the money will roll over from year to year so there is no need to worry about making sure you use it all.

Managing the Costs of Health Care After Age 65 — Medicare

Once you turn 65, Medicare is typically less expensive than your prior health insurance coverage. People younger than 65 who are disabled or who have end-stage kidney disease can also get health care through Medicare. For 2019, Medicare premiums can range anywhere from $135.50 to $460.50 per month for an individual, depending upon whether you'll need the supplemental Medicare plans.

Medicare Part A – Hospital Insurance

Medicare Part A, known as hospital insurance, covers hospital bills, hospice, home health and access to a skilled nursing institution. Part A will typically be free as long as you have been working and paying Social Security taxes for the last 10 years. If not, you will pay a sum of monthly premiums to access Medicare Part A. Once you have qualified for Part A, basically any care and comfort you receive when you are actually admitted to the hospital is covered, minus deductibles and co-pays.

Medicare Part B – Medical Insurance

Medicare Part B, known as medical insurance, includes everything that is deemed "medically necessary" but does not require hospitalization. Common services, such as outpatient preventative care, checkups, X-rays, laboratory and ambulance services, etc. are included. Unlike Part A, Part B does have a monthly charge. This is an amount determined by the date you enroll and your income. If you are enrolling in Part B for 2019, here's what you'll pay:[19]

If your yearly income in 2017 (for what you pay in 2019) was:			
Individual tax return	Joint tax return	Married and separate tax return	You pay (in 2019)
$85,000 or less	$170,000 or less	$85,000 or less	$135.50
$85,000 to $107,000	$170,000 to $214,000	Not applicable	$189.60

---

[19] Medicare.gov. Centers for Medicare & Medicaid Services. "Part B costs." https://www.medicare.gov/your-medicare-costs/part-b-costs/part-b-costs.html.

$107,000 to $133,500	$214,000 to $267,000	Not applicable	$70.90
$133,500 to $160,000	$267,000 to $320,000	Not applicable	$352.20
$160,000 to $500,000	$320,000 to $750,000	$85,000 to $415,000	$433.40
$500,000 +	$750,000 +	$415,000	$460.50

One last thing: Part B has a penalty! If you don't apply for Part B when you are first eligible and try to enroll later, you will be penalized. Your monthly premium may go up 10 percent for each full 12-month period that you could have had Part B. This does not apply to folks who choose to work beyond age 65 because they are covered by their current employer. But, if you do not have coverage from a current employer or the U.S. Department of Veterans Affairs and you elect not to join Part B, you will be penalized in the future if you decide to join.

Medicare Part C – Medicare Advantage

Medicare Part C is also known as Medicare Advantage (MA). The basic premise of MA was to create an alternative to the original Medicare law by allowing private insurance companies to become the primary care providers. These Medicare-approved private health insurance plans are for individuals who are enrolled in original Medicare Parts A and B.

These MA plans must cover all of the services that original Medicare covers, except hospice care. In addition, they may offer extra coverage, like prescription drug coverage, vision, hearing, dental and/or health and wellness programs. They also may allow you access to a wider range of health care personnel and facilities.

If you decided to join a Medicare Advantage plan, you must continue paying the premium for your Medicare Part B, in addition to the MA plan premium.

Medicare Part D – Prescription Coverage

Medicare Part D adds prescription drug coverage to original Medicare, as original Medicare does not cover most medications. These plans are offered by insurance companies and other private companies approved by Medicare. Medicare Advantage plans may also offer prescription drug coverage that follows the same rules as Medicare prescription drug plans.

There are many different types of plans. Some have deductibles and some do not. Some have co-pays while others have co-insurances. Since each plan can vary in cost and the list of drugs covered, it's important to choose the right one for your needs.

As with Medicare Part B, if you do not enroll in a Part D plan when you are first eligible and do not have creditable prescription drug coverage, you may have to pay a late enrollment penalty.

Rising Cost of Health Care

While Medicare costs may be a little more manageable, we can expect that over time these costs will consistently increase, and not just at the normal consumer price index. Health care inflation is a completely different rate. Recall the inflation charts in the Income Avenue chapter? Health care inflation is typically much higher than the regular consumer price index inflation rate.[20]

---

[20] US Inflation Calculator. Updated March 13, 2018. "Historical Inflation Rates:

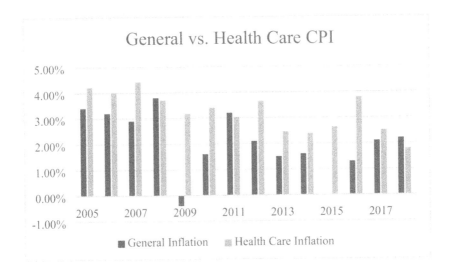

Another significant aspect of health care after you turn age 65 is, from that point on, you can re-analyze your insurance on an annual basis and make changes regardless of your health status. Think of it as an annual contract.

You can analyze your insurance annually to determine if the type of coverage you have is still adequate for your needs at that time. If it's not, you can upgrade. If you feel you are overpaying for what you need, you can reduce or change your coverage and expenses. This is something that you can actively manage the cost of, if you take the time to do so.

For 2019 Medicare coverage, open enrollment was from Oct. 15, 2018, to Dec. 7, 2018.[21] During open enrollment, you can make the following changes:
- Change from original Medicare to a Medicare Advantage plan and vice versa.

1914-2018." http://www.usinflationcalculator.com/inflation/historical-inflation-rates/
[21] Medicare Resources. 2018. "FAQs: When Is the Next Medicare Open Enrollment Period?" https://www.medicareresources.org/faqs/when-is-the-next-medicare-open-enrollment-period/.

- Switch from one Medicare Advantage plan to another MA plan.
- Switch from an MA plan that doesn't offer drug coverage to one that does and vice versa.
- Join a Medicare prescription drug plan.
- Switch from one Medicare drug plan to another.
- Drop your Medicare prescription drug coverage completely.

Long-Term Care

When it comes to long-term care, no matter how much you pay or what kind of health care insurance you have, one key point to remember is you usually have 100 days. The minute you leave a hospital, whether you go to a rehab facility or receive home health care, you're looking at about 100 days of coverage. Whether you are over or under age 65 and have Medicare or an employer-sponsored plan, your coverage will be approximately the same — 100 days.

After the 100-day mark, your care will be considered chronic or long-term care. Long-term care is what you need if you can no longer perform everyday tasks by yourself due to a chronic illness, injury, disability or the aging process. It is chronic care that you might need for the rest of your life. You can receive it in your own home, a nursing home or another long-term care facility, such as assisted living.

Long-term care is a very thorny problem, and there aren't any silver bullets. Whether you need nursing home care, assisted living, or you prefer to receive home health care, there are a number of different strategies for addressing your long-term care needs.

1. Self-Funding

The first and most basic strategy is self-funding. Self-funding is basically setting aside assets to pay for your care. How much do you need to set aside in case you need it? According to the "Genworth 2018 Cost of Care Survey," the median annual cost of a semi-private room in a nursing home in 2018 was $89,297. In the same study, they have estimated the median cost will rise to $161,280 by the year 2038.[22] These costs are even higher in the Northeast. That's some folks' entire retirement savings, which is why self-funding is typically not the best solution for many families who come into our firm.

2. Medicaid

Another planning strategy for addressing long-term care is Medicaid. Medicaid was designed to provide health insurance for the indigent and those on welfare. Some estimates say that as many as seven out of 10 people living in nursing homes use Medicaid — many of them middle-class people who, having burned through their savings, are as dependent upon the program as the people who never had assets in the first place.

While this program was intended for only low-income earners, many individuals who live comfortable lives, own property and have substantial home equity choose to adjust their net worth in order to fit the government's definition of "low income" and thus qualify for Medicaid if they need nursing home care. They must do this financial maneuvering five years before the need arises, however, because these moves are subject to a five-year look back. This "look-back" process is very arduous, and, if you are thinking of using this particular strategy it would be beneficial for you to sit with a qualified

---

[22] Genworth. June 2018. "Genworth Summary of 2018 Survey Findings." https://www.genworth.com/aging-and-you/finances/cost-of-care.html.

financial planner and/or estate planning attorney to go over in detail how it works and what you need to prepare for. Keep in mind, when you are on Medicaid, you are a ward of the state, and they have all the say in where and how you receive care. They are paying the bills, so they make the rules.

3. Life/Long-Term Care Insurance and Traditional LTC Insurance (Underwritten Policies)

The most well-known strategy for paying for long-term care (LTC) is to invest in LTC insurance. However, long-term care insurance is getting very costly and the costs are continuing to rise. Many people are finding it difficult to include LTC insurance as a part of their retirement plan due to the high payments. The good news with LTC insurance is that the old plans that involved paying premiums that we lose if we don't use them are becoming obsolete.

However, if you want to look at this method as a way to shift the burden, you will need to go through medical underwriting. This is a health insurance term referring to the use of medical or health information in the evaluation of an applicant for coverage. Insurance companies will gauge your health to make two decisions: whether to offer or deny coverage, and what premium to set for the policy.

Let's first explore the LTC options that require you to pass an underwriting exam. In order to qualify for the underwritten options, your health needs to be average to above average. Remember, insurance companies that offer these types of coverage are in it for the long haul and are very particular about whom they offer coverage to. If you are in good health, here are some of the options that may be available to you:

Traditional LTC insurance may be a good option for you if you are income rich but cash poor, or if your main asset is real estate. Some policies combine traditional LTC insurance with

Medicaid planning. This is where you hold the policy for the "look-back" period. Then, once your assets transfer into an irrevocable trust, you can drop the LTC policy.

If you use this strategy, it is advisable to seek the assistance of a retirement advisor who is also capable of helping you with your overall retirement planning. It can become a bit more complex than we can detail in this book. Just know that the option exists.

Another benefit of traditional LTC insurance is that it could help protect the equity in your property. For Massachusetts residents, a qualified LTC insurance policy can protect their home from being sold to cover long-term care costs. That being said, a major downside to this strategy is that you pay premiums for a very long time and, if you don't need the money, you lose it.

Life/LTC insurance is gaining ground as a solution to paying for long-term care. Not surprisingly, many folks just were not impressed with the "use it or lose it" approach of traditional LTC insurance. Many people are uncomfortable with the thought of paying $6,000 to $10,000 per year for insurance they may never need. Add 20 years' worth of those premiums together and you have a pretty tidy sum.

It doesn't take the insurance industry very long to react to public opinion. When they discovered that LTC policies weren't selling, the actuaries and computer jockeys who design insurance products went to work. They took a look at the old standby life insurance, LTC's older brother. Here, they observed, was a product that had been around for centuries, had a solid claims reputation, and enjoyed a good history of not raising premiums. As the story goes, two family members got together over a cup of coffee and decided to launch the hybrid life/long-term care insurance that their product engineers had designed. Why? What could a combined plan do? A combined plan could answer the biggest nagging question that the people had. The answer to "What if I never need the care?" was "death benefit." The new hybrid programs would have a death benefit value, which meant that if the insured never needed care, then a tax-free death benefit would go to the beneficiaries. Suddenly, a plan that had no tangible value if it was never used now had real value. It also had a large sum that would be delivered tax free, and probate free, to the insured's heirs.

How do these plans work? These hybrid policies have two pools of benefits: one for long-term care, and one for life insurance. Some programs still have the two pools of benefits, but vary in where they put the emphasis. Some plans are slanted more toward LTC and others are slanted more toward life insurance. Other plans balance the two benefit pools, giving each aspect equal emphasis.

The other large difference between the life/LTC policies is how they are funded. Some policies are funded with one single lump sum premium, which results in what is called a "paid up" policy. Others are funded with a monthly or annual premium. Still others can be paid in 10 years, and then at the end of the 10-year period, the policy is paid in full. Let's explore the single-premium options first.

Single premium options offer two benefits that are striking and set this option apart from the monthly funded options: (1) it becomes fully paid and there is no need for additional funds; (2) *the premium is fully liquid minus surrender charges in the case of emergency.*

Here is an example of how it would work:

For a 59-year-old male nonsmoker with a $250,000 deposit, there would be three buckets:

- $175,000 is fully available for emergency purposes.

• $1.2 million would be available for long-term care purposes.

• $410,000 would be paid, tax free, as a death benefit if long-term care is never needed.

How about a 59-year-old female nonsmoker with a $250,000 deposit?
   • $175,000 is fully liquid at any time.
   • $1.2 million is in the long-term care bucket.
   • $460,000 is in the life insurance bucket.

Both polices would pay for LTC after you were deemed unable to perform two of the six common *activities of daily living* (ADLs): eating, bathing/hygiene, dressing, grooming, mobility and toileting/continence, or if you suffered from cognitive impairment such as Alzheimer's or dementia. Both policies would pay for nursing home care, home health care and assisted living facilities. Both policies' benefits would be reduced by what you used, if you used any of the benefits at all.

Let's say, for example, that you used only $60,000 of LTC benefits. The life insurance bucket would be reduced by that amount, and then the remaining amount would go to the spouse or beneficiaries upon your death.

Note: Some contracts may not have a walk-away feature, but may offer more long-term care/life insurance benefits.

What if your family does not have the $500,000 to put toward a life/LTC policy? Then we would use the monthly funding strategy. The monthly funding strategies do not have the full return of premium that the single-deposit plans have, but they do have some residual value, and the death benefit and the long-term care benefit are exactly the same.

Let's take that same couple who did not have $500,000 to put down, but still wanted the life/LTC insurance plans.

Male and female, 59 years old, nonsmokers:

Their $6,000 per year would buy $350,000 of total benefits for long-term care and life insurance purposes. Should either one of them become unable to perform two out of the six ADLs, or if they suffer from cognitive impairment, they would be able to start drawing down the benefit on a monthly basis. Should either one of them die, the remainder goes to beneficiaries.[23]

The way these policies work, if you never need the long-term care, then the full amount of the death benefit is paid *tax free* to your beneficiary when you die.

Sometimes clients will draw down their IRA money and use all or a portion of their required minimum distributions (RMDs) to fund these types of policies for both LTC and tax purposes. Another option would be to opt for a payment plan that lets you pay your entire insurance policy in 10 years, referred to as the "10 years paid up" plan. For those folks that are still working, this is a great option to consider. This type of plan allows you to make payments for 10 years only, and then by the time you retire, you have the benefit of the life/LTC insurance without having to make any additional premium payments.

4. Non-Underwritten Policies

Whether it is traditional LTC insurance or the hybrid LTC/life insurance policies, both require underwriting because of the possible large payout by the insurance company if you

---

[23] The case studies/examples and results included in this book are for illustration purposes only and may not be typical. The results shown will not be achieved for all clients or even for any client. Results for each client will differ depending on the client's situation. They should not be considered specific investment advice, do not take into consideration your specific situation, and are not intended to make an offer or solicitation for the sale or purchase of any securities or investment strategies. **Investments involve risk and are not guaranteed.** Additionally, no legal or tax advice is being offered. If legal or tax advice is needed a qualified professional should be engaged.

should need the care. But what if you are in poor health and uninsurable? What if you have a history of heart disease, diabetes or cancer? There's good news.

The insurance industry has come up with another way of funding long-term care coverage by designing another hybrid product that is known as the ***LTC/fixed annuity***.

Similar to the single-premium plans, this product requires a significant upfront deposit to make it strong enough to cover health care costs. But there are other uses for this product.

Just like the underwritten combination policies have a life insurance component, the non-underwritten "combos," as they are called by those in the insurance industry, have a traditional fixed annuity component, which is all about income, income, income. In other words, anyone who is considering a traditional fixed annuity for part of the guaranteed income portion of his or her portfolio now has the appealing bonus of an LTC component. This is a very positive trend in the world of insurance. If you need income in retirement anyway, then why not look at a strategy that could double your income should you need long-term care?

Income riders: You can now add what are called "income riders" to annuities, whether they are fixed, indexed or variable. These income riders guarantee a certain rate of return, regardless of the performance of equities (on which the return of variable annuities is based), the interest rate environment (upon which the return of traditional fixed annuities is based) or the index without downside (upon which the fixed index annuities are based). While the account defers, or "cooks," you receive this guaranteed rate, which can range anywhere from 4 percent to 7 percent, depending on the contract you choose. The catch is that, in order to capitalize on this guaranteed interest rate, you generally have to annuitize, and take the value over a lifetime. The lifetime payout can be set up so that it pays on one life, or on joint lives, with the remainder of the account passing on to a beneficiary.

These income riders are a very popular way of setting up a stable retirement income to supplement Social Security. Remember too, that the guarantees provided are based on the financial strength of the issuing company, so make sure that you are comfortable with the insurance company behind it.

Assuming we are comfortable with the company, what has been truly revolutionary is the fact that in the past few years the insurance companies have added an LTC benefit to those same payouts. Now, when a client who is receiving a lifetime income payment is unable to perform two out of the six ADLs, suffers from cognitive impairment, or is confined to a nursing home, the income amount doubles.

> *Here is how it works: John Doe is 55 years old, has $300,000 in a 401(k) from a job he recently left, and he elects to invest in a fixed annuity with an income rider that includes an LTC component. He plans on working and does not need the income, so he elects to defer the income for 15 years until he turns 72. At age 72, he will be forced to make withdrawals from the account anyway due to the required minimum distribution rules set up by the IRS for tax-deferred accounts.*
>
> *Original investment: $300,000*
>
> *Income account value: $893,926*
>
> ***Guaranteed lifetime income:*** *$53,636 (6 percent of income account value)*

---

[24] Please note that there are many different variations on these riders and some may

***LTC doubler:*[24]** *$107,272 ($53,636 x 2)*

Not only does John have the $53,000 per year to live on and to supplement Social Security, he also has the peace of mind of knowing that his lifetime payment doubles if he is unable to perform two out of the six ADLs mentioned previously in this chapter, or if he suffers from cognitive impairment. So now he can use the $107,000 per year to cover the costs of long-term care, whether at home, an assisted living facility or a nursing home.

As you can tell, there are certain factors that enhance this planning tool and make it even more effective, such as making a larger deposit or allowing additional time to defer. The features and benefits of the product also vary by state.

This option is relatively new on the retirement and long-term care planning scene. The best feature of it is that no medical underwriting is required. This should be of special interest for those who have been turned down for either traditional LTC insurance or life/LTC insurance. They now have a place to park money to use for LTC purposes, for income purposes, or both. Perhaps the best part of all is that if they never use it for income or for long-term care, the full asset value goes to beneficiaries and avoids probate. In that respect, it performs just like many other annuities.

Case Example

One client, who was diagnosed with rheumatoid arthritis and atrial fibrillation at age 60, had a family history of needing long-term care. She taught figure skating and was quite active. But

---

not exist at all in the state you live in. Please check with your local financial professional to see which, if any, are available in your area.

because of those two notations on her medical record, both traditional LTC insurance and LTC/life insurance were unavailable to her. So what did she do? She invested $200,000 into a LTC/fixed annuity. Her primary reason was the LTC coverage. Her secondary reason was that she knew she might need income in the future. She regarded the LTC/annuity combination as the perfect "two birds with one stone" solution, and she addressed both issues at one stroke.[25]

From the standpoint of a planner, we cannot emphasize enough how important this development will be to so many people in their search for long-term care solutions. Before this product was introduced, we used to inform those who were turned down by underwriting that there were no other options. That is not the case any longer.

Addressing the Long-Term Care Gap

The gap in LTC costs is enormous and only growing, and the federal government is making it harder and harder to qualify for assistance. What was once a three-year look-back period is now five years. What was once a penalty that was time-stamped is now retroactive and pushed into the future.

Compounding the situation is the "good problem" of increased longevity through medical technology. The number of people lining up for long-term care is multiplying, and we have not yet even seen the baby boom wave crash onto the LTC

---

[25] The case studies/examples and results included in this book are for illustration purposes only and may not be typical. The results shown will not be achieved for all clients or even for any client. Results for each client will differ depending on the client's situation. They should not be considered specific investment advice, do not take into consideration your specific situation, and are not intended to make an offer or solicitation for the sale or purchase of any securities or investment strategies. **Investments involve risk and are not guaranteed.** Additionally, no legal or tax advice is being offered. If legal or tax advice is needed a qualified professional should be engaged.

scene. One major news network called it the "Gray Tsunami," stating that by 2050 the number of people in the world age 80 and older will quadruple. That will spell a financial emergency of immense proportions, with an unprecedented number of people needing expensive long-term care that they, their children, their grandchildren and the government will not be prepared to pay for.

In America, it is projected that most of the current 65-and-above population will need some form of long-term care.[26]

Thankfully, as is usually the case, the private sector has sprung into action and is delivering alternatives and strategies that are redefining how people plan for that care, regardless of their health status, financial status or disposition toward paying premiums and getting nothing in return. Regardless of what strategy you choose, the bottom line is this: choose one. As we mentioned before, do it and do it early. The clock is ticking, and no one we know is getting any younger. There will never be a better time to break out some of the new tools that have expanded our options in addressing the LTC gap.

With health care costs on the rise and many complex insurance options to choose from, having a well-thought-out plan for covering your health care needs is a critical component to your retirement. That's why it is one of the five key parts to our *Retirement Road Map®* process at SHP Financial.

---

[26] LongTermCare.gov. October 10, 2017. "The Basics." https://longtermcare.acl.gov/the-basics/

CHAPTER FIVE

Legacy Planning

For many of today's retirees, it's important for them to pass on assets to loved ones. If your estate plan is not properly set up, the passing of those assets can be a painful, time-consuming and costly process. We don't want that for our own children, and our clients don't want it for theirs, either. That's why legacy planning is the fifth step in our *Retirement Road Map®* process.

Avoiding Probate

When transferring wealth to your loved ones, the ultimate goal is for that transfer to be instant, tax efficient and probate free. Probate is a system administered through the courts that helps in the orderly distribution of your assets after you've passed away. During this process, creditors and various government agencies will be getting their fair share of your estate, too.

You want to avoid probate for many reasons. It is expensive and often billed hourly by attorneys. It can diminish or sometimes eliminate your assets. It's also time-consuming — potentially tying you up for months, even years.

Despite what many people think, assets traveling through the probate court system will not automatically pass on to your heirs, even if you have a will. In fact, having only a will usually guarantees that you will end up in probate. So how can you set up your legacy plan to avoid probate?

1. Proper Beneficiary Designations & Titling

Many types of financial assets allow you to designate a beneficiary. Upon your death, these assets become the property of whomever you designate as the beneficiary, and are no longer a part of your probated estate. First, make sure that all of your assets are property titled and/or have a current beneficiary on them. Many people either have no beneficiary listed or they have failed to keep the beneficiary current. It's very important to review your beneficiary designations and make sure they are up-to-date. Also, be aware that many asset classes do not allow the naming of a beneficiary. Real estate in Massachusetts is one particular example. For assets that do not allow the naming of a beneficiary, consider establishing a trust to own the asset.

2. Hire the Right Attorney

A second way to avoid probate is to utilize the services of an estate planning attorney who does not also do probate. Not every attorney does both, but most do. If you hire an attorney to set up your estate plan and that person also handles probate cases, how can you be certain that this attorney is doing what is in your best interests? The attorney would be making money both on setting up the estate and in probate. If you go to probate, the attorney will benefit and make substantially more money in the process

— your money. Hiring someone who solely handles estate planning but does not handle probate should provide you with confidence that there are no ulterior motives.

3. Consider Putting Valuable Property Into Trust

The third and most significant way to avoid probate is to put your property in a trust. The advantage of holding your valuable property in a trust is that after your death the trust property is not part of your probated estate. That's because a trustee — not you as the individual — owns the trust property. After your death, the trustee can easily and quickly transfer the property to the family or friends to whom you left it without probate. You specify in the trust document, which is similar to a will, who you want to inherit the property.

If you are considering putting assets in trust, beware that not all trusts are the same. If your trust is not set up properly, it may not protect you. It's critical that you work with a qualified estate planning attorney who has extensive knowledge in trusts and keeps up-to-date with the current codes to ensure your trust is set up properly.

Once your trust is set up, the next critical step is to "fund" it. This step needs to involve a financial advisory team that is fluent in trusts and taxes, such as the advisors at SHP Financial.

4. Gifting

For obvious reasons, giving away property while you're alive helps you avoid probate. This also lowers your potential probate costs because, as a general rule, the higher the monetary value of the assets that enter into probate, the higher the expense. However, you must be aware that gift taxes apply if the gift is in excess of a certain amount, so this is typically only a good option if the asset is below the gift tax threshold. For 2019, the annual gift exclusion is $15,000.[27] You must also be aware of how gifting is impacted by cost basis, which we will discuss later in this book.

Estate Taxes

Nowadays people know about the $11.4 million dollar federal tax threshold, the point at which there is a tax on property transferred from deceased persons to their heirs.[28] However, many people do not realize that here in Massachusetts that threshold is much lower. In Massachusetts, the estate tax triggers at $1 million per person or $2 million per couple, and is retroactive back to the first dollar. This includes cash, stocks or other assets as well as real estate and life insurance. Given today's property values, it's much easier for retirees to hit that threshold.

One way to help reduce estate tax liabilities is to put your assets in a trust. As we mentioned previously, putting your assets in a trust can help avoid probate. An added benefit to a trust is that it can also help with reducing estate taxes and protecting your assets from creditors and lawsuits. Homes put in a trust can avoid significant capital gains taxes upon the death of a spouse in some circumstances. However, you should know that not all trusts can do these things. Simply having a trust will not ensure these benefits, rather, you should hire legal counsel that routinely prepares trusts of this complexity.

Another way some estates pass on assets tax free is by using grantor retained annuity trusts (GRATs). With a GRAT, the estate owner puts money into a trust that is designed to repay the estate the initial amount plus interest at a rate set by the U.S.

---

[27] IRS. 2018. "Frequently Asked Questions on Gift Taxes." https://www.irs.gov/businesses/small-businesses-self-employed/frequently-asked-questions-on-gift-taxes.
[28] IRS. 2019. "Estate Tax." https://www.irs.gov/businesses/small-businesses-self-employed/estate-tax

Treasury, typically over two years. If the investment rises in value, the gain goes to an heir, tax free. On the other hand, if the investment does not gain in value, the full amount still goes back to the estate. This can help avoid large amounts of tax when stock or other assets rise in value quickly.

Capital Gains Taxes and Step-Up Cost Basis

When you inherit property, such as a house or stocks, the property is usually worth more than it was when the original owner purchased it. Fortunately, the value of the property is readjusted using a step-up basis. Using the step-up basis, the value of the asset is determined to be the higher market value of the asset at the time of inheritance, not the value it was when originally purchased. This will help to minimize the beneficiary's capital gains tax.

For example, say your grandfather bought a piece of property many years ago for $15,000 and the value has now grown to $250,000. If he sold the property prior to his death, he'd be responsible for paying capital gains tax on the $235,000 profit. However, if your grandfather held onto the property until death, the property will be included in the estate at full market value — potentially skipping capital gains taxes on decades of appreciation.

When it comes to the step-up basis, there is one important note we should mention relative to gifting. We promised we'd get to it earlier and here it is: When a person gives a noncash asset to someone else, the original owner's cost basis carries over to the recipient. So, if your uncle gives you stock shares worth $20,000 that he acquired for $600 many years ago, then your cost basis will be $600 when you sell the stock and you will be responsible for all of those capital gains.

On the other hand, if your uncle left the shares to you upon his death, the step-up basis would apply and $20,000 becomes the cost basis, so there is no tax on the gain of between $600 and $20,000.

Life Insurance and ILITs in Estate Planning

Life insurance can play an important role in an estate plan for many families. It can provide immediate cash for heirs to use for the payment of death taxes, debts, burial expenses and other settlement debts.

However, many people are unaware that life insurance proceeds can be subject to federal and state estate tax, especially if the policyholder has "incidents of ownership" in the policies or if the proceeds are payable to the estate. In other words, the death benefit of the life insurance is includable in the net estate for calculation of the estate tax. To avoid this, you may want to consider giving up ownership of the policy. When giving up ownership, all incidents of ownership must be surrendered or transferred to someone else, such as your spouse, a child or to a trust, and it must be done more than three years in advance of death.

These irrevocable life insurance trusts (ILITs) are often used as an advanced planning technique to provide a source of cash for heirs to pay estate taxes on assets such as property, businesses or other items of value, or to pass wealth to your heirs tax free. While they can provide a number of benefits, an ILIT is a complex legal arrangement that requires professional assistance to ensure it is set up and administered correctly.

Let's take a look at an example similar to one we have seen in our office. Let's suppose a couple, we'll call them George and Linda, are in their early 60s, they're retired, and they have about $1.5 million of assets saved up, $1 million of which is in IRAs.

They have some income coming in from Social Security and other sources, but they'll need to use a portion of their saved assets to generate income. However, even after setting up their income streams, they have a lot left over inside an IRA, which is going to be a huge tax burden on the next generation.

To reduce this tax burden, they're going to utilize life insurance. George and Linda have eight years before they turn 72 and have to start taking required minimum distributions. Their plan is to start paying down their IRA now and putting it into life insurance. For them, if they pay $10,000 a year for the next 10 years, they'll be all paid up and they'll have a $500,000 income-tax-free death benefit for the next generation. Leaving $500,000 tax free behind is almost equivalent to leaving $1 million in the IRA, after taxes. The bottom line is, they'd be able to take $100,000 out of their million-dollar IRA in the next 10 years and leave $500,000 without income taxes to the next generation.

Not only does that maximize their wealth, it also allows them to spend the rest of their IRA assets more confidently in retirement without being concerned about the next generation because they know that they have plenty of assets set aside for them. Even if they spend all of their other money down, they still have a $500,000 tax-free death benefit set aside for the next generation. If they wanted to pay for the policy all at once, rather than splitting it up into 10 annual payments of $10,000, the cost to pay for it all at once is lower, at $85,000. Some people also opt to pay for it over their lifetime. There are many different ways to maximize wealth for the next generation without disrupting your lifestyle during retirement.

There are many different types of policies to consider. It's important to work with an experienced financial planner who can determine your needs for life insurance and assess the types of policies that may be suitable for your particular estate planning needs.

Conclusion

The most important step in legacy planning is to avoid procrastination. No one wants to make plans for what happens upon their death. It's certainly no picnic, but it's a critical part of your overall retirement plan. None of us knows how long we will be blessed to be on this Earth, so it's important to get all of your affairs in order to avoid probate, reduce estate tax liabilities and make life easier for your heirs.

At SHP Financial, we take a holistic approach to retirement planning — making sure that every aspect of your retirement is planned for, including legacy planning. We do not claim to be estate planning attorneys, but we realize the importance of planning for what will happen to your assets and to your heirs upon your death. For the legacy portion of your plan, we work with many great estate planning firms in our state, including Keith McManus of McManus Estate Planning LLC and attorney Matthew Larr of Mass Heritage Law LLC, who were kind enough to provide their valuable insights for this chapter of our book. Once we sit with you and discuss your general needs in this area, we then refer you to an estate planning firm to complete the specifics of this portion of your plan.

CHAPTER SIX

Building Your Own Road Map

Now that you know what your retirement strategy should include, it's important to make sure that you find a financial professional who can deliver and execute this kind of plan. Not all financial professionals are the same, and it's crucial to find the right financial planner for you. The following are some of the key qualities to look for in a financial planner:

1. Accumulation vs. Distribution Advisor

When it comes to financial advisors, there are two kinds: accumulation specialists and distribution specialists. In your early working years, your financial advisor specializes in what we call the accumulation phase. They help you accumulate your wealth and invest it for the long-term to save for retirement. Accumulation advisors, which best describes the bulk of financial planners today, are typically all about growth and risk.

This works well when you have a long time horizon and don't need the money.

However, once you have less than 10 years before you are ready to retire, or if you are already retired, it's time to seek out a financial advisor that specializes in the ***distribution phase***. The distribution phase is when you address the structuring, and in some cases restructuring, of invested assets to provide retirement income for life. Many folks have expressed a fear of running out of money in retirement, and for good reason. Today's retirees are living longer than ever, and it's critical to keep their principal assets safe, which makes the distribution of their assets an essential focus of their planning.

Did you know that most deaths on Mount Everest occur on the way down the mountain, not on the way up? It seems hard to believe, but it's true. According to a 2008 study conducted by Massachusetts General Hospital, most deaths occur during descents from the summit in the so-called "death-zone."[29]

Similar to climbing Mount Everest, accumulating money while you are working is not as difficult a process as it is when you are entering the distribution phase of retirement, or "coming down the mountain." There is much more work and planning that needs to take place to protect your hard-earned assets and ensure that you will not outlive your money.

A good ***distribution advisor*** will have the expertise necessary to help you transition from the accumulation phase to the distribution phase of retirement — when you are ready to put a plan in place to start drawing on the funds you have worked so hard to accumulate.

Although it can be difficult to leave a financial advisor you have developed a relationship with for years, you don't want to

---

[29] Massachusetts General Hospital. Science Daily. December 15, 2008. "Why Climbers Die on Mount Everest."
https://www.sciencedaily.com/releases/2008/12/081209221709.htm.

work with someone who puts you in a portfolio and asks you to sit patiently through bear markets. Once you're entering into retirement, you can no longer afford to do that.

Many people who listen to our radio show have come to our office for a second opinion. They come with their portfolios, but no plan. A portfolio is just a bunch of investments. It's not a plan. It's not even an investment strategy. A true holistic retirement plan, with a detailed distribution, or income plan, is the only real way to give you confidence that you will have enough income in retirement. And, as we have expressed throughout this book, this plan also needs to incorporate strategies for income, investments, taxes, health care and legacy to truly address all of the concerns you will face in retirement.

A key question to ask your current advisor is: "How will we create income in retirement?" What you don't want to hear back is that your advisor will be taking an automatic four percent withdrawal from your savings, adjusted annually for inflation. If you are unlucky enough to retire during a lengthy bear market, like the one we had from 2001 to 2003, you will likely outlive your money.

A financial advisor or planner who specializes in distribution can help you navigate the tough decisions that need to be made in retirement and provide you with a written game plan. This plan, which takes time, effort and professional experience, focuses on several tasks at once: producing income, reducing taxes and growing your portfolio all while minimizing risk and protecting your nest egg. At SHP Financial, we do all of the heavy lifting for you, and our *Retirement Road Map®* plan encompasses all of these key areas: income, investments, taxes, health care and legacy.

2. Independent & Holistic Advisor

Some advisors at large brokerage houses or insurance companies are sometimes trained to fit everyone into one particular program or product. It's all they have to offer and they are trained to think that their product or fund is perfect for everyone. But everyone's situation is different.

By contrast, an independent, or open-source, financial advisor has access to a full array of programs, products and strategies to build a well-rounded, holistic plan. When we founded SHP Financial back in 2003, we knew we wanted to be independent. We did not want to be beholden to a large corporation and force our clients into products that are not right for them. As independent advisors, we are not beholden to any particular product. Rather, we offer a holistic approach to retirement planning with the ability to create a custom plan to fit each client's unique goals and situation, focused on the five key areas of our *Retirement Road Map*®.

When a broker or financial advisor works for a large brokerage firm, they work for the firm, not for you. Their first loyalty is to the company shareholders, not to you, the client. As an independent advisor, we work for you and only you. We represent you, not a company. Our clients are our number one priority, and we go above and beyond to show them.

3. Work With a Fiduciary

As outlined earlier in this book, we highly recommend you look for a financial advisor who is a fiduciary. Not all financial advisors achieve this high standard. This is one of the most important questions you can ask your advisor. In fact, when asked this question, many advisors will tell you that, even though they are not fiduciaries, they still "act like fiduciaries." We caution you not to be fooled by this. It's not the same. To be absolutely sure that you are not being pushed products or investments with unnecessary fees, or that are not right for you, it's important to have an advisor who is bound to make decisions that are always in your best interest.

As fiduciary advisors at SHP Financial, we are obligated to put your interests first, thereby offering more value and transparency. We're held to a higher standard. Knowing your financial advisor is a fiduciary will give you an added sense of confidence knowing that every aspect of your plan is designed to benefit you, not them.

4. Find Someone You Can Trust

It's crucial to find someone you can trust, and who will be there for you, managing your plan, for the rest of your life. What if you passed away? Who would be there to help your spouse? Who would be there to help your children? How do you know whether or not you can trust someone?

First, do your homework. Before you go to an initial meeting, research the firm online. Look at their website. Do they offer educational information? Do they seem helpful and knowledgeable? How have they established their credibility? Are they Certified Financial Planners?

At your first meeting, pay attention to how the advisor interacts with you. The advisor should ask a lot of questions and demonstrate good listening skills. If the advisor talks more than he or she listens, that could be a sign of trouble. You need someone who really listens, who cares about you and demonstrates a desire and ability to help — someone with whom you have good chemistry. It's also a good idea to ask for references and call their clients to see how happy they are with their service before and after their plan has been implemented.

5. **Adequate Staffing**

Finding a firm that has an appropriate level of staffing is crucial. You don't want to work with an advisor who does not have enough support staff behind him or her to adequately take care of your needs. There is a multitude of behind-the-scenes work that needs to be done to put together, implement and then manage your retirement plan for the rest of your life. If your advisor does not have the proper team in place, he or she will be spending more time pushing paperwork and less time managing your money. Also, what if your advisor retires or suddenly needs to leave the business? Would he or she have an adequate team in place to take care of you?

At SHP Financial, as of 2020, we have over 900 clients we actively work with, and it's our top priority to make each and every client *feel* that they are our top priority. That requires a team. Currently, we have six advisors and over 20 additional staff members to help manage our clients' accounts, and we continue to look for exceptional quality people to add to our team as we continue to grow.

Paving the Way to a Beautiful Retirement

We consider retirement precious. We consider *your* retirement precious. Your retirement is the culmination of every single sacrifice you've made. It's all the years of hard work day in and day out throughout your life. It's every frigid January morning you had to wake up, scrape off your car and get yourself to work instead of staying warm in bed at home. It's every gorgeous summer day that you spent inside at work instead of relaxing on the beach, playing golf or doing pretty much anything other than having to go to work. Your retirement is about all of these sacrifices you have made over the years.

That's how we see your retirement. We know how important it is to make sure these assets are protected.

Planning and managing our clients' retirement plans is something we take very seriously. As outlined in this book, a solid retirement plan needs to micromanage every aspect of your retirement, including income, investments, taxes, health care and legacy. The considerations outlined here are just the beginning. There are so many more details that need to be addressed, and you don't have to do it alone. We can do it for you. We're here to help you put together your *Retirement Road Map*®, and we'll be there with you every step of the way, readjusting the route for any detours that may arise — so you can enjoy your retirement years without having to worry about your financial well-being.

ABOUT THE AUTHOR

Matthew Peck, CFP®, CIMA®

Matthew obtained his Certified Financial Planner, or CFP®, certification in 2015, is a member of the Financial Planning Association®, and, through the Chartered Institute of Management Accountants, is a CIMA® qualified professional since 2019. He is insurance licensed, and holds his Series 65 securities license, which allows him to provide financial and investment advice as a fiduciary advisor. As a fiduciary, he is required to avoid conflicts of interest, operate with full transparency and always do what is in the best interest of his clients.

Matthew is author of the book "Mind the Gap: The Cracks in the American Retirement System," and for about a decade he has co-hosted the popular financial radio show, "The Retirement Road Map," which airs on Boston's WBZ, WRKO and WXTK.

Matthew, his wife, Diana, and their four children currently reside in the storied Ashmont Hill section of Dorchester, Massachusetts — not far from the Savin Hill neighborhood where he grew up. Graduating from the award-winning Boston Latin School in 1996, Matt went on to earn cum laude honors from the University of Connecticut in 2001, where he was awarded the dual degrees of Bachelor of Arts in history and Bachelor of Arts in English. In 2015 he earned Boston University's Certificate of Financial Planning. In 2019, he earned the Wharton School's designation of Certified Investment Management Analyst.

Certified Financial Planner Board of Standards Inc. owns the certification marks CFP®, Certified Financial Planner™ and CFP® in the U.S., which it awards to individuals who successfully complete CFP Board's initial and ongoing certification requirements.

The CIMA® certification signifies that an individual has met initial and ongoing experience, ethical, education, and examination requirements for investment management consulting, including advanced investment management theory and application. To earn CIMA® certification, candidates must: submit an application, pass a background check and have an acceptable regulatory history; complete an in-person or online executive education program through a registered education provider; pass an online certification examination; pass a second background check; and have three years of financial services experience at the time of certification.

CIMA® certificants must adhere to Investments & Wealth Institute's Code of Professional Responsibility, and Rules and Guidelines for Use of the Marks. CIMA® designees must report

40 hours of continuing education credits, including two ethics hours, every two years to maintain the certification.

ABOUT THE AUTHOR

Derek Gregoire

In 2003, after receiving a finance degree and working several years in the retirement income planning field, Derek Gregoire co-founded SHP Financial with the mission of providing independent and innovative financial strategies for retirees and pre-retirees, as well as providing customer service that is above and beyond industry expectations.

Derek is insurance licensed, and holds his Series 65 securities license, which allows him to provide financial and investment advice, as well as personally manage investment portfolios as a fiduciary advisor. As a fiduciary advisor, he is required to avoid conflicts of interest, operate with full transparency and always do what is in the best interest of his clients.

Unlike many financial advisors and wire houses who focus solely on investments, Derek has always believed that our clients deserve more. He realizes the critical importance of using all of the available tools and strategies to create the best possible retirement plan for his clients. That's why he and his partners chose to be independent. As an independent wealth advisor, Derek is not limited to what he can offer. He works with his clients to create holistic retirement plans that focus on five key areas of retirement: income planning, investment management, tax optimization planning, health and long-term care planning and estate planning. We call this unique, trademarked planning process the SHP Retirement Road Map®.

Due to his skills, abilities and sound retirement planning strategies, Derek was recognized by Boston Magazine as one of their "Top Wealth Advisors" in February 2010 and was recently nominated for the 2018 SouthCoast Emerging Leader awards.

For about a decade, Derek has been host of the popular "SHP Retirement Road Map Radio Show," which airs on WBZ, WRKO and WXTK each weekend.

Derek has also been seen on local network affiliates of NBC, CBS, ABC and FOX and has been featured in several national publications such as Kiplinger, Forbes magazine, The Wall Street Journal, USA Today and Newsweek.

Derek is also one of 36 contributing authors to the book "Victory: Winning in Health, Wealth & Success."

Derek graduated cum laude from the University of Massachusetts at Amherst with a degree in finance. He's active in the local community — working with organizations such as the Plymouth Council on Aging, Cranberry Hospice/Jordan Health Systems and the Dana-Farber Cancer Institute. He is devoted to his Christian faith, loves playing and watching sports and has a newfound love of golf. Derek currently resides in Lakeville, Massachusetts, with his wife and two boys.

ABOUT THE AUTHOR

Keith Ellis

In 2003, Keith and his partners co-founded SHP Financial—a financial firm focused on providing independent, unbiased financial planning for retirees and pre-retirees.

Now, for over two decades, Keith Ellis has been helping clients preserve and protect their assets, allowing them to enjoy what they have worked so hard to accumulate throughout their retirement years.

Keith is insurance licensed, and holds his Series 65 securities license, which allows him to provide financial and investment advice, as well as personally manage investment portfolios as a fiduciary advisor. As a fiduciary advisor, he is required to avoid conflicts of interest, operate with full transparency and always do what is in the best interest of his clients.

Unlike many financial advisors and wire houses who focus solely on investments, Keith realizes the critical importance of using all of the available tools and strategies to create the best possible retirement plan for his clients. That's why he and his partners chose to be independent. As an independent wealth advisor, Keith is not limited to what he can offer. He works with his clients to create holistic retirement plans that focus on five key areas of retirement: income planning, investment management, tax optimization planning, health and long-term care planning and estate planning. We call this unique, trademarked planning process the SHP Retirement Road Map®.

Keith is co-host of the popular "SHP Retirement Road Map Radio Show" which has been airing for about a decade on various local radio stations including WBZ, WRKO and WXTK each weekend.

Keith has also been seen on local network affiliates of NBC, CBS, ABC and FOX, and has been featured in several national publications such as Kiplinger, Forbes, The Wall Street Journal, USA Today and Newsweek.

Keith Ellis is also one of the 36 contributing authors of the book "Victory: Winning in Health, Wealth & Success."

Keith earned his bachelor's degree from Franklin Pierce University with honors, and currently resides in Sagamore Beach, Massachusetts, with his wife and three children. With his busy life, he still devotes time to various charities, including the Plymouth Council on Aging, Cranberry Hospice/Jordan Health Systems and the Dana-Farber Cancer Institute.

ACKNOWLEDGMENTS

Primarily, I would like to acknowledge the CFP Board of Standards, which helped develop the idea that financial planning was less about picking "hot stocks," rather it was about providing solid and ethical advice to the clients in myriad ways. This book is emblematic of this movement to provide context and goal setting to the critical parts of an individual's financial household: income planning, investment planning, tax planning, health care planning and legacy planning. Without understanding all of the components, the advisor is groping in the dark for the right solutions.

This too extends to the client who also may be in this same hindered position. I would like to thank each and every reader of this book for beginning the process of financial literacy and illumination.

Lastly, I would like to acknowledge Becky Levesque, who helped spearhead this effort to condense and publicize our process. Without her patience and fortitude, this project would never have been completed and the book you are reading would not exist.

- Matthew C. Peck, CFP®, CIMA®

ACKNOWLEDGMENTS

I have to first acknowledge my Lord and Savior Jesus Christ. Because of Him, I have true meaning in life.

I also have to acknowledge my mother and father. They sacrificed so much to give my sisters and me a great life; their hard work should be an example to all, and their dedication to each other and to the Lord is an inspiration.

I also like to acknowledge my beautiful wife, Kylene. We met in college and she has always stuck by my side. Our two wonderful boys, Paxton and Camden, keep me excited about life every day. I am very proud to be a dad and husband!

Keith, Matt and I would like to thank attorney Keith McManus of McManus Estate Planning for his contributions to the Legacy Planning chapter of this book, and for taking great care of the clients we have referred to him.

Next, I would like to acknowledge my business partners Keith and Matt. It is not too often that you can find two people who share similar values and integrity, and, God willing, I look forward to working with both for years to come. And last but not least, thanks our amazing staff. We would not be the company that we are without all of you!

- Derek L. Gregoire

ACKNOWLEDGMENTS

I have to first acknowledge God for putting me in the position to positively affect so many people and families. This is the reason we do what we do.

I would also like to thank my parents, especially for the values they have instilled in me, like being respectful, caring and having a strong work ethic. I hope I can be half the parent to my two boys they were to me.

I'd also like to acknowledge the most unbelievable person in my life, and my best friend, my wife. Maura is an incredible mother to our two boys.

Derek and Matt, people say partnerships don't last. We keep bucking that trend and I could not imagine doing this with two better people. You guys are two of my best friends. It makes things easy.

I would like to also thank the most unreal group of people that anyone would want to work with: our staff. They are second to none, and we're fortunate to have these special people in our lives. AMAZING!!

Finally, I would like to thank the people who are taking the time read this book. It means so much and we cannot thank you enough.

- Keith W. Ellis Jr.